A-Z Sociology Coursework Handbook

COMPLETE

AZ

Sociology

Coursework

HANDBOOK

Joan Garrod
Anne Clynch
Tony Lawson

3rd edition

Hodder & Stoughton

A MEMBER OF THE HODDER HEADLINE GROUP

Orders: please contact Bookpoint Ltd, 130 Milton Park, Abingdon, Oxon OX14 4SB. Telephone: (44) 01235 827720, Fax: (44) 01235 400454. Lines are open from 9.00–6.00, Monday to Saturday, with a 24 hour message answering service.

British Library Cataloguing in Publication Data
A catalogue record for this title is available from the British Library

ISBN 0 340 87261 6

First published 1999
Second edition 2001
Third edition 2003

Impression number 10 9 8 7 6 5 4 3 2 1

Year 2007 2006 2005 2004 2003

Copyright © 1999, 2001, 2003 Joan Garrod, Ann Clynch and Tony Lawson

Cover photograph: Stuart McClymont/Getty Images

Typeset by Phoenix Photosetting, Chatham, Kent

Printed in Great Britain for Hodder and Stoughton Educational, a division of Hodder Headline Plc, 338 Euston Road, London NW1 3BH, by Cox & Wyman Ltd.

Contents

How to use this book

The aim of this book is to guide and support you through the task of carrying out your sociology coursework at both AS and A2. It is not intended that you should sit down and read the book at one sitting and it would be of limited use to you if you did.

You will get most benefit from the book if you familiarise yourself with the layout and get a broad overview of what is in the different sections, and then use it as a reference book, reading about what you want to know when you need to know it.

The book is in four main parts:

1   **A section-by-section approach (Sections 1–12) which deals with the various stages of the coursework process, from deciding on the initial title to writing the evaluation and conclusions. Help is also given regarding the best way of presenting your work. While most of this part relates to A2 coursework, AS students will find Sections 7–10, which deal with specific sociological methods, of help to them when deciding which method to select for the research proposed in their coursework task (AQA), or identifying the potential problems of particular methods as part of their research report (OCR).**

2   **An advisory part (Sections 13–16) which deals in more detail with the specific requirements of AQA and OCR coursework at both AS and A2.**

3   **A comprehensive guide to the best use of information and communications technology in coursework (Section 17).**

4   **A support and resources section which provides you with an A-Z glossary of coursework terms, lists of useful sociology websites, and details of organisations which might be of help to you in your search for information.**

In addition, you will find throughout the book several examples of 'Research in Practice', giving examples of extracts from different pieces of coursework. At the end of each of these is a 'Coursework exercise', designed to make you think carefully about some of the important issues raised. Completing these exercises will give you important practice in the kind of things you will have to consider and make decisions about when you do your own coursework, including identifying and solving problems. It is a good idea to work through these exercises with a friend, or in a small group, so that you can share ideas and learn from each other.

As well as checklists covering specific sections of your coursework, on pages 124–127 there is an overall checklist for AQA and OCR coursework at both AS and A2 level, to help you make sure that you have done everything you are required to do for your coursework task.

Introduction

What is 'coursework'?

The word 'coursework' is a general term used to describe a form of assessment in which students carry out a piece of work (much of which is often done outside the classroom) over a period of time. Coursework may be a compulsory element of a scheme of assessment or, in the case of AQA and OCR, an optional element, which students may choose to carry out rather than taking an unseen written examination on the same topic area.

Both AQA and OCR give students the opportunity to undertake coursework in both the AS and A2 parts of the sociology course. In both cases, opting for coursework at AS does not mean that you are committed to coursework at A2. Coursework represents 15 per cent of the total marks for both AS and A2, so students choosing to do coursework at both levels can gain 30 per cent of their total A level mark for sociology in this way.

The coursework option at AS is referred to as the 'coursework task' by AQA and the 'research report' by OCR. At AS, whichever of these two options you choose, you will not be carrying out research, but will be engaged in a structured task to demonstrate your understanding of sociological methods. The AS coursework options for AQA and OCR are described in more detail in Sections 15 and 16 of this book.

A2 coursework options provide you with the opportunity to undertake research into a sociological topic of interest to you, based on primary data, secondary data, or a combination of both. It is, therefore, important to take note of those aspects of your course which you have found particularly interesting, thought-provoking or of relevance to you, and which you would like to explore further. Remember, though, that although you will be researching something of personal interest, you must approach it in a sociological way, and demonstrate all the skills of good sociological research. The research and background work carried out and presented as your coursework or personal study allows you to display important skills in a different context and format to that of an unseen written examination. You should read your specification carefully to make quite sure that you understand the specific requirements laid down by your awarding body. Refer to pages 81 and 89 (AQA) and pages 86 and 113 (OCR) for further information and a summary of the skills which are assessed and the maximum number of marks allocated to them.

OCR students have to submit a formal Research Proposal for approval, while AQA students will negotiate their coursework proposal with their teacher. One of the most important aspects of your research is the need for good planning, which allows you sufficient time to do the work thoroughly. It is therefore very important that you make a note of the various dates by which the different parts of your research project have to be completed. If you are an OCR student you must pay particular attention to the date by which your Research Proposal must be sent to OCR.

Research in Practice

Oslyn had thoroughly enjoyed studying the 'family' as part of her course. She was hoping to do a higher education course in creative writing or some aspect of the media, and her ambition was to become a script writer. She loved the 'soaps', and watched them whenever possible. Oslyn decided to use the work she had done on the different types of family structure to discuss family structures in contemporary Britain, and then analyse the different soaps to see whether the types of family they portrayed showed the same diversity. She also decided to construct a questionnaire to see whether people generally felt that the soaps gave a true picture of family life in Britain today, or whether they presented a distorted version of it. She decided that she would administer the questionnaire to some of her fellow students (though not those following the sociology or media studies courses), some of the teachers, and some other people based on family and acquaintances to try to get a spread of ages. She realised that this would not be a completely random sample, but still thought that it was worthwhile. She decided that she would also write to the major television studios to see whether she could get a reply from the scriptwriters involved regarding their criteria in choosing the story lines and family situations. Did they opt for 'realism', or for what they thought would make 'good television'?

Coursework exercise

1   State Oslyn's planned research topic in the form of a *hypothesis*.

2   Give a suitable *source* for Oslyn to obtain statistical data on family structures in contemporary Britain.

3   Suggest a reason why Oslyn decided to *exclude* sociology and media studies students from her research.

Coursework is far from being a 'soft option', but can bring you enormous benefits. It provides useful insights into sociological theories and methods, and allows you to experience what being a sociologist is all about. There are no easy options or substitutes for hard work and careful planning, but if you follow the guidelines and suggestions in this book and do the recommended tasks given to help you acquire the necessary skills, you should be able to feel confident that you will submit the best possible work of which you are capable.

A B C D E F G H I J K L M N O P Q R S T U V W X Y Z

How to get started

Deciding what your coursework research should actually be about can be quite difficult. Some people have so many different ideas they can't choose between them, while others find that their minds stay stubbornly blank. Good sociology project ideas will usually come from one of the following sources:

1 An aspect of a sociology topic that you have enjoyed. For most students, this essentially limits the research area to whatever topics have been studied in the first year of your course.

2 The research proposal you designed for your AQA AS coursework task or the subject of your OCR research report. You might decide that you want to carry out the research exactly as you planned it at AS, but in the light of the additional sociological knowledge and understanding you have acquired since then, you may wish to adapt it in some way, perhaps by modifying the hypothesis or aim, or changing an aspect of the research method.

3 Something you have seen/read in the media which provides scope for sociological research and analysis. For example, your study of sociology may have aroused an interest in general issues of gender, class, power, ethnicity or culture. You may then be able to use one or more of these concepts to explore one of a wide range of issues. For example, you might wish to research the power of the media to create stereotypes, social class differences in leisure pursuits, or the influence of different types of music or dress on youth sub-cultures.

4 A link between sociology and another subject you are studying. History, English literature, government and politics, art and media studies among others may suggest things which would lend themselves to sociological research and analysis. For example, you might wish to study the portrayal of 'childhood' in art, the economic role of women in medieval England, the structure, aims and achievements of a particular pressure group, or the extent to which advertising creates ideas of a 'desirable lifestyle'.

5   An issue or event in your local community, such as the proposal to build a new bypass, or the lack of suitable facilities for a particular age group, or the growth in the fear of crime – any of these could form the basis of a good piece of sociology coursework.

6   Something arising from your own life which triggers the desire to explore it sociologically and in a wider context. This could be something in your part-time job, such as the pressures on A Level students to take on part-time work, or a company's strategies to socialise workers into accepting corporate norms and values. It could also be something following on from an event in your family – an elderly relative having to go into care, someone being made redundant, or becoming a single parent – any of these could lead to a good project. The most important thing to remember, however, is that while the 'trigger' event or situation is personal, the context and research as a whole must be thoroughly sociological, and not simply anecdotal.

Research in Practice

At one of her family's many social gatherings, Alpana was sitting listening to her grandmother, great-aunts, and some of her aunts talking about their experiences when they had first left India to come to settle in Britain. Despite their laughter at some of the things they had found strange and amusing, it was obvious that in many ways life had been difficult for them.

Although Alpana had heard many of the stories before, she suddenly realised that she was thinking about them in a different way, which she now knew was a sociological way of thinking. She was in the process of deciding what to do for her research study, and thought that she might use members of her very large family to study the experiences of a group of first-generation immigrant women from India. Alpana thought that she could explore issues of culture, to see how differences in cultural norms and practices between the country of origin and the host country were experienced and dealt with. For example, what adjustments did the women have to make, and how did they cope with these? How much of their own cultural norms, values and practices were they able to retain in

Continued

Britain, and were there any difficulties arising from this?
Alpana decided that when she went back to college on
Monday she would do some background research in the
library, to see what sociological literature there was on
this general topic, and then she would discuss her ideas
with her sociology teacher, to see whether they were
worth pursuing.

Coursework exercise

1   Apart from the ones mentioned, what sociological *concepts* can you
    think of which Alpana might use in her research?

2   If Alpana's proposed project went ahead, of what *kind* of research
    study would it be an example?

3   Briefly discuss the *advantages* and *disadvantages* for Alpana in carrying
    out her proposed research.

How to decide on a research focus/title

You will find it helpful to have a focus for your research as early as possible. This focus can take the form of a title which will guide you to a specific area in the specification. It gives you and the reader a framework within which to approach your coursework and provides a summary of your research interest. Students following the OCR specification are obliged to present a provisional title for their personal study to OCR before starting their research.

2.1 Ethics

It is absolutely crucial that, right from the start, you check to see that your proposed research falls within the ethical guidelines. The following is a brief summary of the ethical guidelines issued by the British Sociological Association (your teacher will have a full copy of these). You should apply these guidelines throughout the whole research process, and check at every stage that they are not being breached:

1   **Don't expose yourself or your respondents/participants to any risk, whether physical, social or psychological. For example:**
    i   **don't do primary research into areas of criminal behaviour such as drug-taking, shoplifting or domestic violence**
    ii **don't ask people personal questions on areas which could cause them distress, such as the death of a spouse or childhood abuse**
    iii **never conduct interviews or surveys without someone knowing where you are, and avoid any location which might put you at risk, such as going into a stranger's home to conduct an interview, or doing a survey late at night.**

2   **You must obtain the 'informed consent' of those you are studying. This means that you must make sure that they understand the purpose of the research and its background (i.e. a piece of sociology coursework) and agree to take part.**

3   **You must explain the use to which any findings will be put.**

4   You must explain what you mean by 'confidentiality' and 'anonymity'.

5   Be particularly sensitive when dealing with vulnerable people, e.g. the elderly and young children.

6   Both in your approach, your questions and your writing up, avoid any expressions which could give offence, e.g. those which are sexist, racist, ageist or homophobic.

7   While your teacher needs to know the people or organisations you are using for your research, you should reassure participants that their identity will not be disclosed in the written project (see point 4) and should ensure that this is adhered to.

8   To avoid any possible problems arising from the Data Protection Act, any personal details stored electronically (e.g. on a computer database) should be anonymous. In practice, this means that people on an electronic database should be identified only by a number, and you should keep a written list if it is necessary for you to be able to match the individual to the database entry.

Research in Practice

Ann had a part-time job in a supermarket, where she had worked for a couple of years, and was well-known to the staff. As part of her study of the sociology of work, she had been learning about alienation, and also some of the strategies adopted by employees to 'get round' some of the more irksome rules and make the job more interesting and enjoyable. Having done quite a lot of background reading on the topic, she decided to do a covert participation observation study of her fellow employees, to see whether there was any evidence that they were adopting particular strategies at work.

However, having gone through the ethical guidelines, and discussed her idea with her teacher, she decided that she should not do this as she would be unable to obtain the 'informed consent' of her fellow-workers. However, she still liked the idea of basing her coursework on her job, so she decided to try something different. She decided that she would focus on the effect on family life of female

Continued

workers working part-time and shift work, in particular looking at the possible strains on women with young children, and what adaptations other family members made, in particular husbands/partners, to cope with the situation. Did the partners of such women undertake a greater domestic role than they had previously, for example? Ann decided that she would gather her data by informal, unstructured interviews, and compare her findings with the sociological literature on the topic of the domestic division of labour.

Coursework exercise

1   Suggest a suitable *hypothesis* that Ann might use for her research.

2   Why might Ann prefer unstructured interviews to questionnaires?

3   Suggest two *sources* regarding the domestic division of labour which Ann could use as context.

2.2 The working title

Note that it is acceptable to change your title part way through your research in order to clarify its focus. This often happens on the research journey as students gain a better understanding of the process and are more able to crystallise their thoughts and sharpen their focus on a particular aspect of the topic under study.

It is important to understand the difference between a title and the hypothesis/aim and objectives of your research (see page 12). An example of a title might be:

'Differences in educational achievement between ethnic groups.'

It is clear from this title on which area of the specification you are focusing. Teachers, organisations and participants involved in your research can get an idea of what you are doing and how they may be able to help you. So – how are you going to decide on your title? There are three key issues to consider before making a decision.

1 A title must signal the *area* of research on which you are going to focus

This may seem obvious to most readers but in fact some pieces of coursework submitted have misleading titles. Others are confused, muddled or unclear. Examples of such titles are – 'Women, War and Wimps' and 'Teenagers, The Problem Years'. Both these titles attempted to be snappy but lost the opportunity to be informative. The first one, 'Women, War and Wimps' was too broad and failed to reflect the real focus of the research, which was actually a study of the role of women in the armed forces in 1998. The second one lacked a clear sociological focus from the outset. It sounded as though it could be the title of a self-help book for parents, an article in a magazine or even an area more suitable for research by psychology students. The actual research explored the role of youth subcultures in the inner city, but you would never have guessed this from the title. It is important to ensure that your title signals the sociological area or concepts you are going to explore in the body of your research. 'Sexy' titles may attract initial interest but only sociologically informed ones sustain it.

Another reason for choosing a working title which makes your research focus clear is that in order to gain certain information, you are likely to need to contact an outside person or organisation, perhaps to obtain some secondary data, or to gain permission to carry out an interview or administer questionnaires. It is important for you that the people you contact will be willing to help you, and consider that the time they will be investing will be worthwhile. One of the first things you are likely to be asked about, or which you should indicate if the approach is by letter, is what your research is about. It is essential, therefore, that you agree a working title with your teacher before you make contact with any outside person or organisation. The willingness and ability of outsiders to help you is a good indication of the appropriateness of your working title and, indeed, your research focus.

2 The initial title should be reasonably open

This means that it should enable you to select and employ relevant theories, concepts, empirical studies and statistical data from a range of appropriate sources. It should also provide the scope to call upon different aspects of the specification to inform and further develop your research focus (see context box, page 33). In this way the candidate who focused on 'The role of women in the armed forces in 1998' was able to call upon pertinent concepts such as socialisation, patriarchy, cultural capital and stereotype to develop the theme of her research. Details from feminist research were used to provide a context for the study. The ideas presented were evaluated via other perspectives as well as from within the feminist perspective.

3   A title should give you scope to explore your interests

Most students study three subjects at A Level. Many sociology students bring their knowledge and understanding of social structures, processes and theoretical explanations of social phenomena into other subjects. For example, concepts such as patriarchy, role allocation, power and inequality can be used to interpret themes, characterisation and plot in texts studied in English literature. Such concepts can also help our understanding of historical events and enable us to analyse the messages and images portrayed in the media. This cross-fertilisation of information and transfer of skills is good and will help develop the evaluative style which enhances all work. So students taking sociology and media studies may effectively use some of their media studies material to develop sociology research on, for example, 'The stereotypical presentation of teenagers in magazines'. Students studying English literature and sociology have carried out secondary-source based research to present coursework on 'A sociological analysis of *Lord of the Flies*' and 'A Feminist interpretation of Margaret Atwood's novel '*The Handmaid's Tale*'. Other students, following psychology and English language as well as sociology, have explored linguistic codes and social class differences. However, if you are going to use your knowledge of other subjects to inform and develop your research then it is very important to ensure that:

i   you use *sociological* concepts, themes, research and theories to provide a context for your research and in this way demonstrate a sociological imagination

ii   the focus is a sociological one and the ways in which you interpret and analyse your findings demonstrate *sociological insight*

iii you do not hand in a version of your English, media studies or psychology coursework and hope to pass it off as sociology. You are likely to end up with no marks if you do this, as the mark scheme rewards *sociological* knowledge, understanding, application and analysis.

Research in Practice

Kate was studying sports science and psychology as well as sociology. She decided to use knowledge and insights from her other two subjects to inform her sociology coursework. She had been reading about how many women are dissatisfied with their body shape, and she decided to explore whether female athletes, by virtue of being fit and trim, had higher self-esteem with regard to their body shape than non-athletic women of the same age. Kate knew that she would have to explore issues such as the social construction of 'beauty', the role of the media in portraying and emphasising a 'desirable' female body-shape, and feminist views on the pressures put on women to conform to such ideals. Kate realised that she would have to interview female athletes and non-athletes to be able to come to a conclusion, and would be able to use her sports science contacts to get a sample of women athletes. She felt confident that, although her studies in sports science and psychology would help her, the research and its underlying ideas and concepts would be entirely sociological in nature.

Coursework exercise

1 Suggest a 'working title' for Kate's research.

2 Explain what is meant by 'the social construction of beauty'.

3 Suggest how Kate might explore this aspect of her research.

4 Suggest how Kate's studies in psychology might be of help in her research.

Finally, remember that initially, all titles are working titles. Choosing an effective working title will enable you to explore theories, concepts and studies and collect potentially relevant material from a variety of sources. As you become clearer about the precise nature and focus of your research, you are nearer to deciding on a final title.

2.3 What is the difference between a working title and the final title?

A working title provides focus during your research process (or research journey), particularly in the early stages. It may change a few times because of your reading of sociological studies (secondary source material) or analysis of data. It may change after discussions with your teacher, as it was initially too narrow or too broad. It may also need to change because it was insufficiently sociological to reflect the concerns of your research or satisfy the marking criteria which will be used to assess your research.

Remember that the final title will be the one which will appear on the front cover of your research project. It will influence the examiner's expectations of what will be inside. It is also likely that on reaching the end of your coursework the examiner will return to the front cover (OCR personal study) or to the Candidate Record Form (AQA coursework) to make sure that your research falls within the area defined by the title. The examiner will be looking to see if the title informed the rationale (see page 26) and translated into the working hypothesis/aims and objectives which then guided the research process. Make sure, then, that your final title provides a source from which your hypothesis/aim and objectives can emerge naturally.

Research in Practice

Mohammed started work on a project entitled 'Inequalities in the workplace'. This working title helped him to provide a preliminary focus for his research. He was able to contact personnel officers (one at his father's firm and one where he had a part-time job) to ask if he could visit them to discuss his research. He knew that both companies had a large workforce. He was also able to write to the Equal Opportunities Commission for information in this area. His teacher helped him learn how to use the Internet and CD-ROMs to search for useful references.

After reading some of the information he had gathered, he was able to reduce the scope of his research. He decided to focus on 'the number of people from minority groups in promoted posts, and an examination of aspects of institutional racism at work'. He realised that this could

Continued

be very sensitive research and he would have to be careful to follow the BSA ethical guidelines if he were to pursue it.

However, the personnel officers, on hearing the nature of the research, said that they were now unable to help, so Mohammed changed the focus again. This time he decided to examine the extent to which students under 18 years of age with part-time jobs felt that they were exploited at work. He got the personnel officer's permission to compare the type of work done and the hourly rates of pay of part-time student workers and permanent full-time employees. The personnel officer also gave permission for him to use the staff rest room to carry out interviews with different employees.

Coursework exercise

1 Suggest why Mohammed's initial working title would be unable to be sustained throughout the research process.

2 Suggest why the title 'An examination of aspects of institutional racism' would prove difficult for a student wishing to carry out primary research.

3 What *ethical* issues are raised by the proposed research into 'the number of people from minority groups in promoted posts and aspects of institutional racism'?

4 Suggest a working title for the project which Mohammed finally decided to research.

How to decide on your hypothesis/aims and objectives

By now you will know that a clearly stated hypothesis or aim and precise objectives will influence the success of your coursework. They are the driving force of your research. They also play the very important function of bringing together the different parts of your research and thus give coherence to the finished project. So from the start your hypothesis/aim and objectives should emerge from your working title.

It is important to know the difference between these three terms.

a **Hypothesis.** This is a testable statement or possible explanation. You then collect data which you will analyse to see the extent to which it supports or refutes your hypothesis. An example of a hypothesis would be: 'Men are more likely to be convicted than women for similar offences.'

b **Aim.** This is a statement of intent to research a particular sociological problem, e.g. 'To investigate the relationship between gender, ethnic group and crime statistics.'

c **Objective.** This is a specific task which you set yourself to do during the research process, e.g. 'To examine statistics relating to male and female crime'.

You should decide firstly whether you wish to state the possible outcome of your research. If yes, then formulate a hypothesis. You should also have at least a couple of objectives to help structure your research. You should make sure that your objectives follow on from your hypothesis and working title, giving you the scope to explore further the issues which emerge from your chosen focus. You may prefer to have an overall aim, together with objectives which help you break down your aim into manageable parts.

After you have translated your working title into a hypothesis or aim and objectives, you then progress them through the context, methodology and content sections of your coursework. In the final section of your project you evaluate the extent to which your research explored the tasks you set yourself in the rationale. The research journey is never complete. Good researchers note any design flaws in their research and ways to improve the rigour of their research. In the final section of your research, the evaluation, you will return to the concerns of your rationale, make recommendations for refining and improving the quality of your research tools or/and offer alternative methodology. Examiners will reward you for doing this as it demonstrates an ability to assess the strengths and weaknesses of your research and to suggest ways to improve on this in future research (see page 73).

Research in Practice

Jane set herself an 'aim' to prove that 'inequalities and patriarchy exist in society'. She quite liked the sound of this as it used sociological concepts, hinted at feminist theory and Jane thought it would impress the examiner. At a meeting with her teacher Jane quickly realised that this was neither an aim, an objective nor a measurable hypothesis and she would have difficulty progressing it within the restraints of A level coursework. This was too broad even to be a working title as it was too open and unwieldy to research. Jane was set the following tasks:

- to choose a topic from the specification which she had enjoyed and one which had addressed issues of inequality
- to narrow down the area and focus on one aspect of inequality which allowed her to explore feminist accounts of patriarchy
- to see how she could then reduce the area further, and formulate a hypothesis which she could test
- to set herself at least two precise objectives which she could follow through in her research.

She produced the following:

Hypothesis

'Women carry out more domestic duties in the home than men even when both partners are in full time employment.'

Objectives

1   To locate and read sociological research on the domestic division of labour.

Continued

2   To investigate the division of labour between couples in full-time employment.

3   To investigate the division of labour between couples where the woman is a full-time housewife.

4   To investigate the division of labour between couples where the woman is in part-time employment.

Jane had felt bogged down with her first suggestion for research because she couldn't see a way forward. She could now be selective in the material she gathered and check that it related to conjugal roles and the division of labour. Notice how it is now easier for her to define the parameters for her context section. She decided to employ a feminist explanation for the division of labour and looked for empirical studies which both supported and challenged her hypothesis.

Coursework exercise

1   Suggest some suitable *studies* which Jane might use in her research.

2   State the sociological *concepts* which would help Jane in her research.

3   Suggest the *method* you think that Jane should use to conduct her research into the domestic division of labour. Give reasons for your answer.

4   Draw up a *questionnaire* or *interview schedule* which you think would be appropriate for Jane to use.

5   Take Jane's hypothesis about the domestic division of labour, and re-state it as an *aim*.

Remember that a hypothesis is a testable statement. So, at the end of her research, Jane should be able to state whether the primary data she has collected and analysed support or reject the claim she made in her hypothesis.

In deciding whether to have a hypothesis or an overall aim, you must choose which best suits you and the focus of your research.

Coursework exercise

1 Look carefully at the list below. Copy it and write in the box against each one whether you think that it is a hypothesis or an aim.

Statement	Hypothesis/Aim
People may not go to church as often as in the past, but they still have religious beliefs.	
To investigate the reasons why some people join ecological protest groups.	
To explore the relationship between violence on television and violent behaviour in society.	
Higher education tuition fees are adversely affecting working-class applications to university.	

2 Take any two of the above statements, and suggest (a) a working title and (b) at least two objectives for each.

3.1 How to prepare yourself for research tasks

There is much work to be done before you write up your coursework. The closer attention you pay to the advice given below, the more likely you are to achieve a good grade for your coursework. A crucial difference between a student who enjoys the research process and completes their research to a high standard and one who doesn't is how organised they were from the outset. Remember – organisation liberates! So although there may be ten months between reading this chapter and submitting your coursework it is essential to:

- **keep a detailed research diary (see page 16)**
- **read and follow BSA ethical guidelines when carrying out your research (see page 4)**
- **read this book carefully before you start the relevant section of your coursework**
- **use the glossary at the back of this book if you come across terms you do not understand**

- read examples of A Level coursework available from your sociology department

- read the Chief Examiner's annual report which describes good and poor practice in students' coursework (your sociology department should receive one each year)

- have an action plan and try hard to stick to it

- regularly discuss your ideas, problems, possible solutions and sources with your teacher and peers

- learn to use a word-processor (including saving your work on disk and making back-up copies), and how to access the internet and use CD–ROMs (see chapter 17)

- make draft copies of each section of your research and be willing to make changes

- make and keep detailed records of useful contacts, copies of all letters you send or receive, and notes of telephone conversations

- keep details of all references and sources used as these will have to be listed in the bibliography

- show your teacher all letters you propose to send out, particularly when using the school/college address, and get approval before the letters are sent

- never plagiarise from texts – it can get you disqualified.

Although it might seem time-consuming, following the advice provided here will save you a lot of time in the long run. It will also contribute to producing coursework which meets the marking criteria, demonstrates qualities found in good research and avoids duplicating the poor practice for which some students have been penalised.

3.2 The research diary

Keeping a research diary is required by both AQA and OCR. It is an easy thing to do as you go along your research journey, and is absolutely vital. It is impossible to remember all the ideas, problems, solutions, contacts you had and used whilst carrying out your research. You cannot create a diary at the end of the process!

OCR states that the research diary 'should be a record of the student's research activities, with comment and reflection on how the investigation process developed in the light of experience, and what was learned from the experience.' AQA's Principal Moderator strongly advises students to keep a research diary which reflects the research process undertaken, identifies sources used, problems experienced, notes possible solutions and, where appropriate, considers alternatives. The contents of a research diary should offer sufficient detail of each stage of the research process to provide material to enable you to evaluate your research journey in a structured, rigorous and informed way in the final section of your report. If you have not kept such a diary, writing your evaluation section will be very difficult. Some students have produced fictitious or factually inaccurate accounts of the research process they undertook because they did not start, or keep, an adequately detailed research diary.

Some students may be competent in the use of, and have access to, an electronic diary and planner (see page 143). For those who don't have, or prefer not to use, electronic diaries, a possible framework for developing a manual diary is provided below. You should however adapt this to suit your own preferred way of keeping track of your research period. OCR students are given instructions to write their diary on A4 paper and ensure that it is enclosed with their study. AQA students will find it helpful to use an exercise book with ruled columns across two pages. Be warned – loose pieces of paper get lost!

3.3 General rules for keeping a research diary

1   Start your research diary from day 1 (but if you haven't, start it now!).

2   Always date the entry.

3   Update your diary regularly.

4   Provide sufficient detail to inform your evaluation section.

5   Leave space after each entry so you can add to it if and when appropriate.

6   Always take your research diary to meetings, e.g. where you discuss your research with your teacher, noting down all comments and advice, and when you visit an outside organisation.

7   Create a section in your diary (at the back of the exercise book is helpful) for details of secondary sources you come across, to enable you to provide a full and accurate reference/bibliography. Fill in all details of the source as soon as you find it. This saves hours going back

to the library or resource centre searching for something you know you read and which you now wish to use or refer back to. You may not eventually use all the sources you note down, so another useful aid for writing your bibliography is to put a large tick against those sources you actually use in your research.

8   Keep another, separate, section in your exercise book for all contacts, giving details of the contact person's name, address (with post code), telephone number, fax number and, if applicable, e-mail and website.

3.4 Research diary in progress

Table 3.1 on pages 19–21 shows part of a research diary which will be added to as the research progresses. You may wish to adapt this example to suit your needs, focus and style of research.

Note that the student started the diary before the summer holidays. She will use the summer holidays to read around the area and prepare for her context section. Over the summer she will keep a record at the back of the exercise book of all sources read, and add to them throughout the next six months.

Table 3.1 An example of a research diary in progress

Research diary for sociology coursework

Working title: Girls and the masculinity of science

Date	Ideas	Problems	Possible solutions	Sources	Comments	Coursework section
June 1	Enjoyed education and differential achievement. Will re-read textbooks, handouts and class notes for focus for research.	Need a working title – take A–Z advice, read section again.	Look at Kelly's research on gender and science. Wonder if it still applies with National Curriculum and all that. Perhaps try something along lines of 'Girls and Science'.	Kelly, DES survey 1980, Whyte 1980, class notes. Put details in sources section of book.	Choice between this one and research on family.	Rationale and Context
		Education and differential achievement too broad even for working title. Need to define focus more.			Decided to go with Girls and Science. Met with teacher 8/6/98 and agreed area. She advised going through past copies of *Sociology Review* and using newspapers on CD–ROM and Internet search for recent material. Put targets for next meeting in my action plan.	Rationale and Context
	Also enjoyed work done so far on family, especially symmetrical families. Will re-read all material I have on this topic.	Might be more work; also difficult to get families involved in my research.	Could look at different structures of family today – perhaps do 'conjugal roles' or maybe family structures in multi-cultural Britain.	Willmott & Young; *Sociological Review*; Anderson; Bott, Oakley.		

A B C D E F G H I J K L M N O P Q R S T U V W X Y Z

Table 3.1 continued

Date	Ideas	Problems	Possible solutions	Sources	Comments	Coursework section
June 22	Need to decide on hypothesis and objectives. Read section in A–Z for guidance. Could have aim instead of hypothesis, but feel this might be too broad. What ethical considerations do I need to think about?	My school is all-girls, so need to contact local college and co-ed school(s) for suitable population. Need to get year 11 pupils involved in my research. Need to visit a college and speak to their students. Need to draft a letter and get it checked by my teacher. Need to decide what methods I will use.	Hypothesis: 'Despite recent changes in education, boys are more likely than girls to opt for science subjects post-16' 1 To see if more boys than girls opt for science at A Level/GNVQ Advanced. 2 To examine range of science text books for stereotypical images and language. 3 To interview science teachers (male and female) to obtain their views on topic. 4 To see if more boys than girls do single science subjects at GCSE.	M Stanworth (*Gender and Schooling*); D Spender (*Invisible Women*); L Culley (*Gender differences and Computing*) – might be something relevant; statistics on subject choices in 'Social Trends'. Also check out WISE (Women into Science and Engineering) and GIST (Girls into Science and Technology) programmes and materials.	Met with teacher 9/7 and agreed a hypothesis and 2 objectives. She advised me to be more precise. We agreed to use A Level/GNVQ students and Y11 as population. Need to sort out sample. Discussed things to do prior to going to schools/college and how to make best of visit.	Rationale and Methodology

Table 3.1 continued

Date	Ideas	Problems	Possible solutions	Sources	Comments	Coursework section
		Haven't got copy of BSA ethical guidelines.	5 To see if students' attitudes towards their science teachers influenced subject choice and achievement at GCSE and A Level.	Get copy of BSA guidelines from department resource room.		
Sept 8	Have a hypothesis on subject choice at A/GNVQ Level and gender. Have two objectives: 1 To examine any differences between a co-ed 6th form college and an all-girls 11–18 in post-16 choices and gender. 2 To investigate gender differences and the taking of separate science or dual science at GCSE, and relate these to post-16 choices.	Need to make appointments and check out method before I go in to institutions. I need to find a school that offers single as well as dual science options. Girls generally do better than boys at GCSE, so this might be a variable I may have to consider when choosing my sample.	Will try the local 6th form college, the girls' grammar school, the boys' grammar school and the local comprehensive to see which institutions will allow me in to collect information.	Get addresses from Yellow Pages. Get teacher to check out letter and see if I can use my school's address. Go to resource centre to type letters. Decide to wait until I get replies from these institutions to see which ones will help and then I will narrow down the population and decide on my sampling frame and method.	Met with teacher to discuss draft letter. It was too long and detailed so we amended. Decided to phone institutions to get the name of the Head of Sociology to send letter to with a SAE enclosed. Need to set up preliminary meeting.	Rationale and Methodology

A B C D E F G H I J K L M N O P Q R S T U V W X Y Z

Table 3.2 Example of a reference section at the back of a student's research diary

Author	Title	Year	Publisher/Journal/Volume
Sharpe, S	Just Like a Girl	1994	Penguin
Greenfield, TA	Gender and Grade Level	1997	Science Education 81/3

Table 3.3 Example of a contacts section

Organisation	Equal Opportunities Commission
Contact name	Ms J Smith (Research Officer)
Address	Arndale House Arndale Centre Manchester M4 3EQ
Phone number	0161 8388269 Fax number 0161 8388312
e-mail address	info@eoc.org.uk Website address www.eoc.org.uk
Dates contacted	27 June
	11 July

3.5 Drawing up an action plan

You are nearly ready to start thinking about drafting your rationale. However before you do this you should first draw up an action plan. You may wish to create a section in your research diary for your action plan, or you may have a system in college/school where action planning and setting targets is routine and timetabled. Either way it is an excellent way to keep on track and ensure you are meeting internal deadlines. It will also enable you to make the most of the time you and your teacher spend discussing your research and agreeing achievable targets for the next meeting.

Table 3.4 An example of part of an action plan for sociology coursework

Targets	Strategies for meeting target	Completion date/comments	Done
• Decide on an area to research	1 Make an appointment to see teacher and discuss area	June 1st	✔
• Create an action plan and take to teacher	2 List areas I've enjoyed – just in research diary	June 1st	✔
	3 Use A–Z examples to help	June 1st	✔
• Set up research diary	4 Look up examples of A Level coursework in department	June 1st	✔
• Agree with teacher a working title for research	5 Design a working title, hypothesis and objective for each area to take to meeting with teacher	June 1st	✔
• Discuss suitable secondary sources	6 Take research to meeting with teacher	June 1st	✔
• Learn how to use CD–ROM, Internet	1 Enrol for CLAIT class or enrichment option	June 1st	✔
• Check software available and learn to use	2 See IT department for personal password and sign Internet agreement	June 1st	✔
	3 Visit Resource Centre – get technician to help with CD–ROMs	June 1st	✔
• Do some background reading for reference	1 Read chapters 1, 2 and 3 in A–Z Handbook	July 23rd (only read 1 chapter in text)	✘
	2 Visit college library to go through *Sociology Review* for relevant articles	Can't take *Sociology Review* out of the library, need cash to photocopy the article	✘
	3 Access Internet and surf for up-to-date material	Can't work Internet – need help, and all terminals were in use	✘

A B C D E F G H I J K L M N O P Q R S T U V W X Y Z

Table 3.4 continued

Targets	Strategies for meeting target	Completion date/comments	Done
	4 Put all sources and contacts made to date in research diary exercise book		✔
• Learning efficient ways of using the Internet	1 See IT Technician, make appointment to book a terminal	July 26th – couldn't find technician, went to Upper 6th leavers do!	✗
• Get copies of 4 articles in *Sociology Review*	2 Get Lilian to help me: arrange date with her	Arranged Aug 7th to go to Lilian's house and use her computer	✔
• Draft rationale	1 Use A–Z guidelines for rationale and questionnaires	Sept 6th (didn't get to the library and only drafted rationale over the holidays). Need to make an appointment to see teacher, check out rationale and agree new targets	✔
• Do background reading for draft context	2 Visit library and work on sociology coursework for 5 days during summer holidays		✗
• Draft pilot questionnaire	3 Do coursework task in A–Z on rationale section and discuss my answer with Sumera		✗

✓Checklist 1
Am I ready to start?

	Completed	
	Yes	No

1 Have I started the research diary with headed columns drawn up? ☐ ☐

2 Have I created a 'contacts' section and filled in details of contacts already made? ☐ ☐

3 Have I created a 'reference' section and filled in references found to date? ☐ ☐

4 Have I read the section on ICT in chapter 17?

5 Have I checked out some sociology websites from the list starting on page 215? ☐ ☐

6 Have I checked what software and CD ROMs are available at school/college? ☐ ☐

7 Have I set up an Action Plan with headed columns? ☐ ☐

8 Have I looked through the list starting on page 205 to see whether there are any organisations which might be of help to me? ☐ ☐

A B C D E F G H I J K L M N O P Q R S T U V W X Y Z

The rationale

This is a brief but very important section of your research. It is where you set the framework for your research and the criteria by which it is marked. The rationale is where you say what you are going to research and why you are researching it. You should also use it to give some indication of how you are going to conduct your research. The examiner will continually refer back to your rationale, asking the same question: 'Has this student researched what she/he said they would?' It doesn't matter if the data you collected contradict your hypotheses. It *does* matter that the hypothesis/aims and objectives you set yourself in the rationale are developed and carried forward.

A rationale should contain:

* **a succinct explanation of the reasons for carrying out the study**
* **a statement of the central research issue translated into a manageable hypothesis or aim, and related objectives**
* **an indication of your preferred design and methodology.**

The rationale should inform each section of the coursework and you should always refer back to it (in terms of your hypothesis/aim and objectives) to illustrate the ways in which your research carries forward the task you set yourself in the rationale. In this way your hypothesis/aim and objectives will feature throughout your whole coursework. In the final section, the evaluation, you will then be in a position to assess the extent to which you have rigorously examined the hypothesis/aim and objectives you set at the beginning of your research journey.

The mark you achieve for your rationale section can not be decided until the examiner has read *all* your project. The marks are allocated for the way you relate your rationale to each section of your coursework. Your rationale is therefore the theme which runs through the entire coursework.

4.1 The three stages of drafting your rationale

Reasons for choosing your research focus

Firstly you should inform the reader of the reasons for carrying out your research. They may be numerous, but be succinct, choosing the most compelling ones. Your preliminary observations, expectations and values should also be briefly noted. In writing about these, be sure to use some sociological concepts, identify central issues for your research, and demonstrate sociological awareness. (You should not digress from the task at hand with anecdotes or lengthy explanations of why you are interested in certain issues in sociology.) In this way the examiner will quickly see that you have a good knowledge and understanding of the chosen area and are able efficiently to select and apply appropriate sources and methodological tools to further your research interest. Whilst most students choose to carry out primary-based research, excellent coursework is possible which makes use of only secondary sources. If you are taking this option, you should indicate in the rationale your reasons for choosing to do secondary-based research.

Research in Practice

Mary was particularly interested in Durkheim's theory of suicide. She also noted that the press claimed that the teenage suicide rate at the start of 2001 was rising. She wondered if this was true. She also wondered if Durkheim's explanations for suicide were helpful in understanding teenage suicides in the 21st century. It was obviously not possible to interview suicide victims and it would be highly unethical to go to their families with intrusive questions. After a meeting with her teacher, Mary decided to do research which was based solely on secondary sources. She made good use of official statistics, comparing data over a period of time, and used electronic newspapers and the Internet to find articles and other statistical data. She used Durkheim's theory to help interpret, analyse and evaluate the data and possible reasons for teenage suicide. She found critiques of Durkheim helpful in evaluating both his theory and her analysis of why teenagers commit suicide.

Coursework exercise

1   Suggest an overall *aim* for Mary's research.

2   Give four *sources* which Mary would find useful to her research.

3   Identify two *problems* with making comparisons from different sets of statistical data.

4   Identify two problems of which Mary should be aware when using *newspapers* as sources of information for her project.

Methodology

Secondly you should provide brief details of your preferred methodology, with reasons for that preference. Do not be too ambitious. Examiners do not want you to use lots of different methods. In fact, it is preferable if you use only one. You can gain full marks by applying one method rigorously, and assessing its usefulness as a research tool in addressing your hypothesis/aim and objectives.

In the methodology and evaluation sections of your report you have the opportunity to demonstrate your knowledge and understanding of appropriate alternative methods for your research.

Hypothesis/aim/objectives

Thirdly you should provide a clear hypothesis or aim, and objectives. You need to decide whether you are going to have a hypothesis or an overall aim for your research. You would probably state a hypothesis if you think you already have an idea of what you are going to find. You would be more likely to choose an aim if you were genuinely unsure of what your research would show.

The advantage of setting yourself some objectives is that they break up your research into manageable chunks, and it is easy to refer back to them in the body of your text. In this way you will be able to check that you are pulling your rationale through your project.

The establishment of a clear hypothesis/aim and objectives is central to your whole research. They are the driving force of your research. If from the start you are too ambitious and set more than you can reasonably address, then you will lose marks. The examiner will go back to your hypothesis or aims and objectives and ask the question 'Have they researched *what* they said they would in the *way* that they said they would?' Even if you've examined one or two aspects thoroughly, but left two untouched, you cannot expect to get full marks, as you did not deliver that which you set out to do in your rationale. So be pragmatic. This is A Level research and worth 15 per cent of the overall marks, so set yourself a research task which is achievable in the time and with the resources available to you.

Do not have a hypothesis/aim/objectives which are too broad as they become unwieldy. If you want a hypothesis, make it quite specific. If you want an overall aim be sure that you choose a focus that can be reasonably examined in your coursework. Set objectives which are precise, narrow and clear.

At the end of your rationale section it is helpful to the examiner if you state your hypothesis/aim and objectives clearly. If you have more than one objective (and you probably will) you should number them. This way you can relate back to them and check that you are carrying them forward through each stage of your research journey.

Remember that the rationale lays down the direction your research will take. It therefore requires a great deal of time, thought and discussion.

The dos and don'ts of a rationale

Project dos

- ✓ Keep it brief.
- ✓ Give reasons for your choice of research topic.
- ✓ State whether you are going to do primary- or secondary-based research.

Project don'ts

- ✗ Have an over-ambitious hypothesis/aim and objectives.
- ✗ Digress or become anecdotal
- ✗ Give a detailed account of your methodology.

Research in Practice

Sarah's rationale

I particularly enjoyed learning about differential academic achievement when studying the Sociology of Education. In Year 10 I had a two-week work experience placement in a primary school as a classroom assistant. The school was my old primary school and it was in a middle-class area of the town where most parents had professional jobs. In our local authority we still have the 11-plus and most children who attended my primary school passed the 11-plus and went to one of four grammar schools in the area. Whilst on work placement I noticed that most of the children had an expectation that they would go to grammar school and many had private tuition to give them extra practice and preparation for the 11-plus examination.

Whilst studying social class differences in education we explored concepts such as the self-fulfilling prophecy, cultural capital, linguistic codes and innate ability. I wondered if some of these might help explain why so many children from my primary school went to grammar school. I found the Marxist explanation for differential academic achievement the most convincing.

In order to carry out my research I will employ quantitative methodology using a questionnaire, and also use official statistics to see if there is a relationship between social class and academic achievement. I will visit two schools – my old primary school, and one in the inner city whose catchment area is from a large council estate. My questionnaire will be distributed to parents of children at both schools. Some of the questions will focus on the parents' educational/occupational background, which secondary schools any older children have gone to, and where they expect their younger children to go. This positivistic-based research will give me primary data which I can then use to see if my findings reflect the official statistics and support my hypothesis.

Hypothesis

'Children from middle-class backgrounds are more likely to pass the 11-plus and go to grammar school than children from working-class backgrounds.'

Continued

Objectives

1 To investigate official statistics on social class and academic achievement.
2 To examine a Marxist explanation of social class differences in academic achievement.
3 To design and administer a questionnaire to parents of children at two different primary schools.

Coursework exercise

1 Explain briefly why the concepts of 'cultural capital' and 'linguistic codes' might prove useful to Sarah's coursework.

2 Identify some possible problems with Sarah's wish to ask questions about the parents' educational/occupational background.

3 Suggest a source for Sarah to find suitable statistics on social class and academic achievement.

4 Devise a *hypothesis* and two *objectives* for an A Level sociology project focusing on 'An examination of family structures in television soaps'.

5 Devise a *working title* for an area that you are interested in researching and check that it addresses the three key issues outlined on pages 6–8.

A B C D E F G H I J K L M N O P Q R S T U V W X Y Z

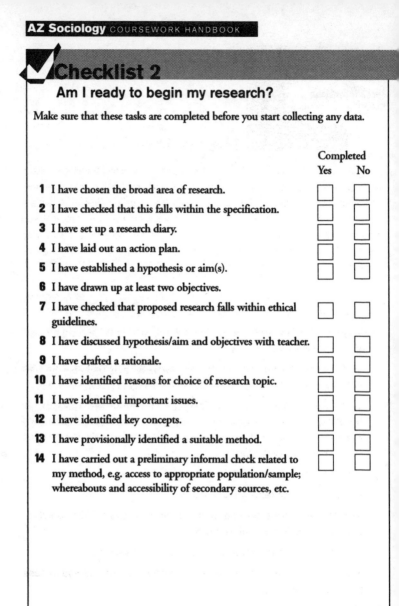

✓Checklist 2

Am I ready to begin my research?

Make sure that these tasks are completed before you start collecting any data.

	Completed	
	Yes	No
1 I have chosen the broad area of research.	☐	☐
2 I have checked that this falls within the specification.	☐	☐
3 I have set up a research diary.	☐	☐
4 I have laid out an action plan.	☐	☐
5 I have established a hypothesis or aim(s).	☐	☐
6 I have drawn up at least two objectives.		
7 I have checked that proposed research falls within ethical guidelines.	☐	☐
8 I have discussed hypothesis/aim and objectives with teacher.	☐	☐
9 I have drafted a rationale.	☐	☐
10 I have identified reasons for choice of research topic.	☐	☐
11 I have identified important issues.	☐	☐
12 I have identified key concepts.	☐	☐
13 I have provisionally identified a suitable method.	☐	☐
14 I have carried out a preliminary informal check related to my method, e.g. access to appropriate population/sample; whereabouts and accessibility of secondary sources, etc.	☐	☐

The context

If you are an AQA student, you will need to provide a context section. This is where you provide the reader with background information on your research, and where you set the scene for your research focus by reviewing relevant secondary source material in the area. Make sure that the material you include in your context section provides the reader with insight into your research focus. This means that you must take care to include only *relevant* sources.

5.1 Presenting a well-planned context section

There is a great deal of planning and work to be done before the context can be written. You need to:

- **read relevant chapters in general sociology texts to help you identify key studies, theories and concepts**

- **visit the resource centre/library and look for articles in newspapers and publications such as *Sociology Review* and *Sociology Update*, which may provide more up-to-date information than the major text books**

- **use the Internet/Intranet to call up useful sites**

- **make use of any relevant CD–ROMs**

- **read the resources section of this book (see page 205) to select and access other useful material**

- **select useful source material and make notes on it**

- **make sure that you always keep a record of sources as you access them (see page 22)**

- **discuss your ideas for this section with your teacher.**

Once you have carried out the above tasks you are ready to draft your context. Remember at all times to be guided by the objectives you set in the rationale.

The following guidelines will help you to present a well-planned and well-written context section. Make sure that you:

- **are succinct**
- **summarise key research in the area**
- **select, explain and apply key concepts (e.g. patriarchy, secularisation, cultural capital)**
- **outline and explain the theoretical context of the study (e.g. feminist approach)**
- **provide, where appropriate, historical and cross-cultural data**
- **make explicit links between the source material and the rationale**
- **evaluate the secondary source material included**
- **identify any trends in the secondary data**
- **refer to any links with the hypothesis/aim stated in the rationale**
- **write a concluding paragraph which summarises the main points.**

The context section provides you with the opportunity to demonstrate the skills which the examiner is looking for. The mark scheme provided by AQA and used by your teacher when marking your coursework allocates marks for each of these skills (see pages 87 and 91). Research which achieves high grades demonstrates all the skills throughout the coursework.

Research in Practice

Maeve found that she was particularly interested in the topic of gender differences in education, and had enjoyed reading the literature. She realised that the introduction of the national curriculum had reduced many of the differences in subject choices made by pupils under 16, and was interested to see whether the differences re-emerged post-16. She received permission from the college principal to obtain details of the students opting for the different post-16 courses in the college for the past three years, and decided to analyse these by gender to see whether any pattern emerged. However, even with government statistical data to make a comparison, Maeve thought that her research needed something more. She therefore decided to go one step further and look at the applications for higher education courses made by her

Continued

fellow students. As well as seeing whether there was again any noticeable gender differences, she decided to explore the reasons why people were choosing particular courses. She wished to see whether there was any evidence that the male students were choosing courses which they thought would make them relatively well-off and successful, and give them high social status, while the females were choosing courses which would enable them to be of some kind of service to people. Privately, she thought that this would not be the case, but considered that it would be interesting to carry out the research. She decided to give a brief questionnaire to all the students in her year who were in the process of making applications to higher education.

Coursework exercise

1   Write a suitable *hypothesis* for Maeve to test.

2   Give two *objectives* which follow from that hypothesis.

3   One of Maeve's sources was a list of the courses chosen by students when entering the college. Suggest one possible *problem* with this data.

The dos and don'ts of a rationale

Project dos

☑ Select only that secondary source material which provides a context for your research focus.

☑ Summarise and edit the secondary source material you use, and leave out anything which is not relevant.

☑ Make frequent links between the secondary source material selected and the stated objectives of your research.

☑ Note the source of information and identify potential bias, e.g. feminist/New Right approach; newspaper ownership.

Project don'ts

☒ Produce a lengthy section which covers most of the research in the topic area.

☒ Digress from the focus of your research, and simply copy pages of data or detail from the source material.

☒ Produce a context section which is an essay and has no explicit links to your rationale section.

☒ Assume that all secondary research is an objective account of the social reality studied, and that all sources are equally valid.

✓ Checklist 3

Have I done my background research?

		Completed	
		Yes	No
1	Have I identified an appropriate theoretical framework?	☐	☐
2	Have I selected and summarised key research studies?	☐	☐
3	Have I read Chapter 17, learned how to use appropriate technology and carried out a search for relevant background material?	☐	☐
4	Have I made a note in my research diary of all sources located/used?	☐	☐
5	Have I prepared a draft context?	☐	☐
6	Have I discussed my context draft with my teacher?	☐	☐
7	Have I checked that my research diary is up to date?	☐	☐

A B C D E F G H I J K L M N O P Q R S T U V W X Y Z

Choosing a method

If you have succeeded in establishing a clear hypothesis or aim, together with some appropriate objectives, you will probably already have some idea regarding which method or methods you are likely to choose to conduct your research. It is vitally important that you look at the relative strengths and weaknesses of each method in the light of what it is that you need to find out. In other words, you are assessing each method in a particular *context*.

Your text books will contain comprehensive details of the range of sociological methods, and their relative strengths and weaknesses, and you must read these carefully and learn them. However, the material in this book is intended to help you focus on particular methods with a view to their potential use in your coursework.

6.1 The stages of choosing a method

Some students start their coursework with a fixed idea of what method they want to use. However, it is advisable to go through the stages indicated below, as they will help you to identify the most suitable method for you in your particular position.

1 What exactly do I need to find out?
This should be your first question. If you have written down suitable objectives which arise naturally from your hypothesis or aim, you will already have a good idea about this.

2 What is the best source (or sources) of this information?
The answers to these first two questions will almost certainly indicate a suitable method, such as a survey, structured interviews, observation, content analysis, etc. At this stage, it is possible that more than one method presents itself as suitable. This leads to your next set of questions.

3   How much time do I have?

Hopefully, you will be planning your coursework well in advance of the deadline, but, realistically, you will have just a few months to collect your data. This will almost certainly rule out longitudinal studies, and should cause you to think carefully about, for example, how many unstructured interviews you could carry out, or how much observation you would be able to do.

4   How much will it cost?

If you had thought of sending out postal questionnaires, you will need to calculate the cost of postage, not only for the original questionnaires and the stamped, addressed envelopes accompanying them, but also for the reminder letters. You will also need to ascertain who will meet the costs of duplicating questionnaires and of any telephone calls you may make — do not simply assume that your school/college will pay. You may also have costs arising from travelling to organisations to conduct interviews, or sending off for information. If you do rough calculations in advance, you are unlikely to have any unpleasant surprises later.

5   How easy is it to gain access to the people from whom I need to obtain information?

The answer to this question is one reason why so many coursework students base their research on their friends, family and fellow students, who provide them with a 'captive audience'! Depending on the topic under study, there are often considerable limitations in using peer groups. However, if you wish to use 'outsiders' instead of your peers, you need to think carefully about both their availability and their likely willingness to help you. There are some fascinating pieces of research which could be carried out using doctors, for example, but few coursework students would be able to gain sufficient access to this group to provide enough information for their study. Other individuals, groups or organisations may be available and willing to help you with your research, but you must consider the time it might take to organise this.

6   What kind of research appeals to me?

Many practising sociologists admit that their personal preferences lead them to favour qualitative rather than quantitative research, or vice versa. It is important to choose a method with which you will feel comfortable.

Your research is likely to go more smoothly and bring you greater satisfaction if you consider all the questions outlined here, and then choose the most suitable method.

Research in Practice

Julie had decided to do a research study based on content analysis. She was interested to see whether there was clear evidence of gender stereotyping in both men's and women's magazines. She had done her background reading for the context section, and had planned to buy four men's magazines and four women's magazines, two weekly and two monthly of each, for a period of three months, as she felt that this would give her a sufficient amount of data to analyse. However, when she came to buy the first set of magazines, she was horrified to find out how expensive they were. She quickly realised that she would not be able to afford the cost of the number of magazines she had intended to analyse, and had to restrict herself to a far smaller number. This meant that, in her evaluation, she had to explain that her conclusions were drawn from a much smaller sample of evidence than she had originally intended. She was annoyed with herself that she had not checked on the cost in advance.

Coursework exercise

1   Suggest two research studies that Julie might have used for her background research.

2   Think of some examples of what Julie might have been looking for in the magazines to see whether or not there was evidence of gender stereotyping.

Using secondary sources

While all coursework will make use of secondary sources, as background research for the context section, some students choose to base their research entirely on secondary sources. AQA provides a separate mark scheme for secondary source-based research. Such types of research include:

* **a critical analysis of a published sociological study**

* **a sociological critique of non-sociological texts, such as novels**

* **a content analysis and critique of an example of contemporary media output, such as television programmes, advertisements, or newspaper stories**

* **an examination and critique of statistical data, such as crime statistics**

* **research based on historical documents, such as diaries, parish registers, or school records.**

Any of these provide rich sources of data, but need very careful thought and prior consideration. Depending on your chosen topic and sources, the following points should be considered:

1 **Particularly if your source material is non-sociological, you must think carefully about the sociological concepts you will need to employ, to ensure a strictly sociological focus.**

2 **While quantity does not ensure quality, ensure that you have access to sufficient material to bear the weight of your research and analysis – you might have problems basing your entire research on one set of statistics, one diary or one old magazine.**

3 **Remember that a significant part of your research will need to be devoted to the *provenance* of your material. This means that you will have to discuss critically the purpose for which it was created, the date it was produced, the audience for whom it was intended, and the background and social status of the creators or compilers of the**

material. You may not have all the information you need or would like regarding these factors, but the issues need to be raised.

Research in Practice

Kevin's father was a churchwarden in the local village church, and through him Kevin knew that their church had exceptionally detailed parish records, going back several centuries. These included not only the parish registers, but also the results of various ecclesiastical censuses. Kevin had been interested in the work of Laslett and Anderson on family structure, and decided to explore this in relation to his own parish. He thought that he would also look to see whether there were any class differences in family structure.

He explained his project to the vicar, who became very interested, and offered not only to allow Kevin to have access to the records, but to help him understand them and read the writing, some of which was very difficult to decipher unless you were familiar with that particular kind of script. Once Kevin saw the huge pile of books involved, he realised that he would have to limit his time span, so decided to look at family size and structure in his village in the period 1750–1800. He decided to look at the age at marriage, the number of children born per family, and, where possible, the structure of households. The vicar told him that this should be possible for at least one part of the period, as there had been a church census which had noted everybody's address. Kevin's village had been, and still was, in an agricultural area, which had been relatively untouched by the industrial revolution. Kevin knew that, if the functionalist view were correct, he should find the majority of people living in extended family households, and having large families, but, from the work of Laslett, he realised that he might well find that this was not the case. He also realised that he would have to supplement his historical research with data about contemporary family structures, to make a comparison. He decided to use data from the last census to do this.

Continued

Having already changed his aims by narrowing his research period, once Kevin started on the documents, he realised that he would have to make another change. He found it impossible to place people accurately in social classes. Most of the householders were listed as some kind of agricultural worker, and he had no way of knowing if there were any important distinctions between them. Also, some of the records were incomplete in this respect. He therefore decided to amend his aims to remove the reference to social class differences, and made a note in his research diary to remind himself to explain this change when writing his evaluation.

Coursework exercise

1   Using the information about Kevin's research, identify two *problems* with using historical records.

2   Suggest where Kevin would be most likely to obtain *access* to data from the latest census regarding his area.

7.1 Content analysis

If you are going to use content analysis in your research, it is important to go about this in a structured and systematic way. You will find it helpful to draw up a grid on which to record the information in which you are interested, which makes it very important to decide on the categories you are going to use. It is a very good idea to test out your categories on a small sample of your chosen material, e.g. one or two television programmes or text books, well in advance, so that when you actually collect your data over your chosen period, you will be properly prepared.

Research in Practice

Ross was studying sociology, English and government and politics, and hoped to train as a journalist. He was very interested by the topic of the role of the media in perceptions of crime, and decided to explore this further. He had noticed a great deal of coverage in his local paper about a series of acts of vandalism around the town centre, leading to a number of letters from people expressing concern about escalating levels of lawlessness among young people. Ross decided to do a content analysis of his local newspaper over a six-week period, to look at how much space was devoted to the reporting of crime in general, and to the reporting of specific types of crime. He would then compare this with the actual distribution of different types of crime in society, using published crime statistics, to see whether there was an over- or under-reporting of certain types of crime compared with their actual incidence. He decided to use the crime statistics to help him draw up his categories, and knew that space in newspapers was measured in column inches. He thought that he would also carry out a content analysis of one national 'quality' and one 'tabloid' newspaper on the same day in each of the six weeks of his data collection, for comparative purposes.

Table 7.1 on the next page shows an extract from the sheets Ross prepared to record his data.

Coursework exercise

1   Suggest a *problem* which Ross might encounter in matching news stories to his crime categories.

2   Suggest a possible *difference* which Ross might see in the types of crime reported in the national press compared with his local newspaper, and give a *reason* for this difference.

Table 7.1 An example of a data record sheet

Type of offence	Number of column inches in news reports: week starting			
	16/10/00	23/10/00	30/10/00	6/11/00
Theft and handling stolen goods (excluding theft of/from vehicles)	6	14		
Theft of vehicles	10	0		
Theft from vehicles	0	12		
Burglary	12	28		
Criminal damage	84	72		
Violence against the person	8	19		
Fraud and forgery	0	0		
Robbery	0	0		
Sexual offences (excluding rape)	0	10		
Rape	0	0		
Drug trafficking	14	0		

Primary data: experiments, case studies and social surveys

Many students base their research on primary data, and the following information should help you to make the most of whichever method you choose.

8.1 Experiments

It is unlikely that you will choose to carry out an experiment for your sociology coursework. However, you may decide that something you have done as a psychology experiment could be adapted for sociology. There is nothing to prevent you from doing this, but there are many pitfalls. Above all else, you will have to ensure that the whole project has a clear sociological focus. As a general rule, you are probably better not taking this approach.

8.2 Case studies

The case study is not 'a method'. It refers to research which looks at a single event or situation in detail. While the usual methods employed are interviews and/or observation, any suitable method may be used. Whether or not you use a case study will depend on the availability of a suitable example at the time you are doing your coursework. The criticism most usually levelled at case studies is that it is not possible to generalise from them. However, provided that you are not aiming to draw general conclusions from your research, this need not be a problem, although you should show that you are aware of this limitation.

Research in Practice

Lucy lived in an inner-city area which, from the residents' point of view, was a 'neighbourhood' with clearly-defined geographical boundaries and a range of local shops and services. Lucy's elder sister was a single parent with a two-year-old daughter, and had worked as a hairdresser before having the baby. Lucy knew that her sister found life a bit of a struggle financially. and often said that she would like to go back to work, at least part-time, if she could find someone reliable to look after her daughter. One day, Lucy's sister came round to say that she had heard that a new childcare day centre was going to open in the area in October, in three months' time. Lucy was interested in the topic of women and work, and knew that many mothers of young children found it difficult to get back into paid employment.

Lucy decided that the timing was right for her to do a case study of the impact of the opening of the childcare centre on local mothers. She decided that she would use the summer holidays to do some background reading on the topic. With the government's emphasis on affordable childcare she thought that there would be a lot of relevant newspaper articles, as well as the material in the text books. She would also conduct interviews with a sample of local mothers with pre-school-age children to find out whether they were planning to take advantage of the new facility, and why. When the centre had been open for a few weeks, she would interview at least one member of staff, and also some of the mothers using the facility. She would also try to re-interview some of the mothers from her original sample.

Coursework exercise

1 State what you think would be an appropriate *aim* for Lucy's research.
2 List at least two *objectives*, drawn from the information above.
3 Suggest one way that Lucy might be able to get the *names and addresses* of mothers of young children in her neighbourhood.
4 If Lucy found that she was unable to obtain the information in this way, explain how 'snowball sampling' might prove helpful, and how she might start this process.

8.3 Social surveys

Planning, carrying out and analysing a survey using a standardised questionnaire is a method popular with many coursework students. It can be a very effective method which generates much useful information, but careful and thorough planning is essential. The following notes will help to guide you through the process.

Sampling

You will almost inevitably use some form of sampling. Think carefully about both the nature and the size of your sample. Some students are over-ambitious regarding the number of questionnaires they hand out or administer, resulting in a huge wealth of data which they are then unable to analyse thoroughly. Be realistic!

Generally speaking, you will want your sample to be *representative*, and you should check and discuss with your teacher the best way of achieving this. If, for whatever reason, you have to adopt a method which is less representative than others, such as snowball sampling, then make sure that you make clear, in the discussion of your methodology, both the reasons for your choice and the potential problems involved.

Research in Practice

Nicos had just watched a fascinating programme on television, about a local launderette and the important role it seemed to play in the community in which it was located. It seemed more of a social and community centre than a place to do your washing, and the people who ran it obviously performed an important function, apart from the obvious one of helping people to have clean clothes! This led Nicos to wonder whether the shops in his own community, a multi-cultural inner-city area, were in any way similar. How important were local shops and services to the local people? How much were they used, and by whom – after all, there were several large supermarkets and a shopping mall just a few miles away. Did the local people have a sense of belonging to a 'community'?

Continued

Nicos decided to carry out a survey, using a standardised questionnaire, of a sample of local people to see how many of the local shops, pubs and other services they used, and why. He thought that he would use quota sampling, as this would be the easiest, and allow him to get a cross-section of people of different ages and ethnic backgrounds. He also decided to carry out in-depth interviews with four local shopkeepers to obtain their views of their community and their role within it.

Coursework exercise

1   **Nicos considered that he could administer questionnaires to 50 people. Draw up what you think would be sensible *variables*, and suggest a quota for each, to make up the sample of 50. (For example, you may think that he should have 25 males and 25 females.)**

2   **State two *disadvantages* of quota sampling.**

3   **Suggest an alternative *sampling technique* that Nicos might use, giving one advantage and one disadvantage of this method.**

8.4 Constructing a *questionnaire*

Writing a good questionnaire which is clear and unambiguous and which successfully elicits the required information is much more difficult than many students think. The following steps will help you to avoid the most common problems.

The questions

1   **Be absolutely clear what it is that you want to find out. Go back to your hypothesis/aim/objectives to establish this, and note it down as a series of points, each of which can be used to form the basis of one or more questions.**

2   **For each area/issue, decide whether the questions will be closed or open-ended. Remember that closed questions force people to respond in line with pre-determined categories, but generate responses which**

are fairly quick and easy to analyse, while open-ended questions allow people to express their own thoughts and ideas and can generate extremely detailed and useful information, but are much more difficult to analyse.

3 Think carefully about the 'personal information' you need to know about your respondents, and ask only for the information which you need to interpret your data. The most commonly-requested details are, of course, sex and age (though it is customary to ask people to put themselves in an age bracket rather than give their actual age in years). Other questions might refer, depending on the topic, to marital status, occupation, number of children, level of educational qualifications, etc. The main point is – don't ask for information that you don't need. If the age of respondents is important to your study, don't make your age brackets too narrow, unless, of course, your study is only of people between certain ages, e.g. 18–30, in which case you may need to have three or four groups between these limits. If you need to know a respondent's occupation, think how you will classify the responses, and either keep the categories very broad, e.g. manual/non-manual, or make sure that you have sufficient knowledge of the occupational structure to use a more refined classification which can incorporate any occupation you may be given.

4 Avoid offensive questions altogether, and be very careful when touching on potentially sensitive areas. For example, asking 'What is your occupation?' could be very embarrassing to an unemployed person, so you might choose to ask for details of 'the current or most recent occupation', or, as some surveys do, include a category of 'unwaged'.

5 Don't make the common mistake of asking 'double' or 'multiple' questions (sometimes known as 'portmanteau questions'), for example 'Which soaps do you watch and do you think that they are over-sensational or fairly true to life?' Keep your questions focused and simple.

6 Try to avoid 'hypothetical' questions. While opinion polls often need to know which party a respondent would vote for 'if there were a general election tomorrow', such speculations are best avoided in your coursework, as it is difficult to assess the reliability of the answers.

7 Beware of 'leading' questions, i.e. those which predispose the respondent to answer in a certain way. Such questions often start with

phrases like 'Don't you think that ...', or 'Wouldn't you agree that ...', thus prompting the respondent to agree with the subsequent statement.

8   Make sure that your respondents are likely to have the necessary knowledge to answer your questions. No-one likes to appear ill-informed or ignorant, and answers which are made up, or large numbers of 'don't know' responses, will not be helpful to you in your research.

An example of a student questionnaire

Attitudes to crime survey

My name is Andrew Mackay. As part of my A Level sociology coursework, I am carrying out a survey into people's attitudes to crime in this area. I should be grateful if you would spare me a few minutes to answer some questions.

Date/time of survey: Date ....   Time ....
Respondent is: Male   ❏   Female   ❏

1   Would you mind indicating which age bracket you fall into?
   (a)   16–21   (d)   50–64
   (b)   22–34   (e)   65–79
   (c)   35–49   (f)   80 and over

2   Have you, or a member of your immediate family, been the victim of a crime in the last two years?   Yes   ❏   No   ❏

3   Apart from your immediate family, do you personally know anyone who has been the victim of a crime in the last two years?   Yes   ❏   No   ❏

4   Below is a list of some different types of crime. Would you place them in the order of frequency that you think that they occur, with 1 being the type of crime you think is the most common, and 6 the type of crime that you think happens least.
   (1)   Robbery   ❏
   (2)   Burglary   ❏
   (3)   Assault/non-sexual violence against the person   ❏
   (4)   Violent sex-related crimes, such as rape   ❏
   (5)   Stealing cars   ❏
   (6)   Criminal damage to property   ❏

5   Do you watch the television programme *Crimewatch*:
   (a)   Whenever it's on/as often as you can   ❏
   (b)   Occasionally – about once a month or so   ❏
   (c)   Hardly ever   ❏
   (d)   Never   ❏

6   Do you watch any fictional British police/detective series, such as *The Bill* or *Inspector Morse*:
    (a)   Regularly/as often as you can   ❏
    (b)   Occasionally – once or twice a month   ❏
    (c)   Hardly ever   ❏
    (d)   Never   ❏

7   With regard to the reporting of real crime by television and newspapers, would you say that the coverage is:
    (a)   too much   ❏
    (b)   about right   ❏
    (c)   too little   ❏

8   Does the fear of crime ever prevent you from going out alone?
                                                   Yes ❏   No ❏

9   If yes, when do you avoid going out?   ....

10 On the whole, would you say that levels of crime in society are:
    (a)   about the same as they were ten years ago   ❏
    (b)   higher than they were ten years ago   ❏
    (c)   lower than they were ten years ago   ❏

11 I would like to compare the attitudes to crime of people living in different areas. Would you mind giving me your post code?

    ....

Thank you very much for your co-operation.

Coursework exercise

1   Suggest what is the most likely *sampling method* that Andrew was using.

2   Give one *reason* why he may have chosen this method.

3   Why do you think that Andrew included the question about *television viewing* in his questionnaire?

4   Why do you think that he left the question about *post codes* until last?

The format

If you are using closed questions, think carefully about the format of the choices you offer to your respondents, and choose the ones that are most appropriate to the question. Some of the most common formats are shown below.

Primary data: experiments, case studies and social surveys

1 A list from which the respondent may choose just one.

For example: Approximately how many times a year do you attend a religious service:

(a) at least once a week ❏
(b) once or twice a month ❏
(c) about 3–4 times a year ❏
(d) once or twice a year ❏
(e) hardly ever/never ❏

2 A list from which the respondent may choose more than one.

For example: Which of the following newspapers do you take in your home on a regular basis:

(a) *The Daily Telegraph*	❏	(f) *The Mirror*	❏
(b) *The Guardian*	❏	(g) *The Express*	❏
(c) *The Independent*	❏	(h) *The Sun*	❏
(d) *The Times*	❏	(i) A local newspaper	❏
(e) *The Daily Mail*	❏	(j) None of these	❏

3 A list which respondents have to place in rank order.

For example: Place the following list of qualities of 'a good teacher' in order of importance, with 1 as the most important and 5 the least important:

(a) Good disciplinarian ❏
(b) Thorough knowledge of subject matter ❏
(c) Always prepares lessons thoroughly ❏
(d) Makes lessons interesting ❏
(e) Friendly and approachable ❏

4 A scale.

For example: For each of the statements below regarding possible features of a good news programme, indicate where you would place it on a scale of 1–5, where 1 is extremely important to you, 3 is quite important and 5 is not important at all.

Covers international as well as national affairs	1	2	3	4	5
Explains the background to the stories	1	2	3	4	5
Comprehensive sports coverage	1	2	3	4	5
Deals with economic issues	1	2	3	4	5
Deals with government policies	1	2	3	4	5
Covers controversial issues	1	2	3	4	5
Has stories about royalty and well-known personalities	1	2	3	4	5

Question order

An important aspect of questionnaires sometimes overlooked by students is the order in which questions appear. You can save yourself some time by writing each question on a separate piece of paper and then arranging them in different orders until you find the best sequence. If you are word-processing your questions, you can do the same exercise using the 'cut and paste' facility.

Final check

When you have a completed questionnaire, read the questions through again carefully, or ask a friend to do it for you, to check that you have not used any sexist or racist language, or included questions likely to cause embarrassment, distress or offence.

You should also draw up a summary sheet for the recording of the replies. Although this must, of course, be comprehensive and cover all questions, you should keep it as clear and simple as possible.

Research in Practice

Eric came home from school one day to find his mother and a group of women from the neighbourhood busy making signs and posters. When he asked what it was about, he learned that they had formed a protest group to campaign against the use of a chemical plant some ten miles away to reprocess low-grade nuclear waste. Listening to some of the tactics they were planning, Eric was amazed. His mother had been a full-time housewife since Eric and his sister had been born, and she had never seemed at all interested in politics, and had certainly never taken part in any kind of demonstration before.

Eric was fascinated by what to him seemed to be a most unlikely band of 'eco-warriors', and decided to explore the issue of different forms of political participation, and the reasons behind them. Using work he had done as part of the 'power and politics' part of his course, he decided to draw up a list of different kinds of political activity, from voting in general elections, through to writing to MPs and

Continued

local councillors, and on to signing petitions, and finally taking part in direct action such as his mother and her friends were planning. Eric thought that he would construct a questionnaire which would enable him to classify the degree of 'political activism' of his respondents, and analyse the responses to see whether any significant features emerged. For example, were the most politically-active people more likely to be of a particular sex, age or class? Were some people only spurred to action by a particular 'single issue', such as that motivating his mother? How high was the level of political activism generally – was it true that most people were fairly apathetic, and sometimes didn't even bother to vote?

Coursework exercise

1   **List four sociological *concepts* which Eric would find useful in his research.**

2   **Using the information in the box and your own knowledge, draw up a list of *'political activities'* which Eric could use in his questionnaire to gauge the level of political activism among his respondents.**

The pilot study

With any questionnaire or interview schedule, you should always carry out a pilot study to test its suitability. This is your best (and usually only) opportunity to see how long it takes to administer, to ensure that all your questions are clear and unambiguous, to see whether there are any questions that could be removed, and to check that you haven't left anything out. It is no help finding out at your analysis stage that there are other details you needed, or other issues about which you would have liked information – it will be too late to do your study over again.

Another important aspect of the pilot is the analysis of the data. You should already have prepared a summary sheet for recording the responses, and should use the data from the pilot questionnaires to check to see how long it takes you to record the information from each one. This may lead you to realise that you have asked for more information than you can easily cope with.

Distributing the questionnaires

This needs careful thought and prior planning, as you may have to obtain permission, for example if you wish to distribute questionnaires in your school or college. Remember that you are likely to get a higher response rate if you administer questionnaires personally than if you post them or give them to somebody else to hand out for you.

If you use postal questionnaires, you will need to write a suitable accompanying letter which explains the purpose of your research, and which gives the date by which you want the questionnaires to be returned. Don't give respondents too long – a week to ten days should be sufficient. You should also enclose a stamped, addressed envelope. Keep a list of all the people to whom you have sent a questionnaire, and cross them off the list as they are returned. If you are not asking respondents to write their name on the questionnaire, you will need to have some sort of a code written on the questionnaire or the envelope so that you can keep track of which questionnaires are still outstanding at the end of your allotted time. You should make at least one attempt to obtain the outstanding questionnaires, either by a follow-up letter, or a telephone call. Research has shown that there are differences between people who return questionnaires and those who do not, so it is worth your while to get as many in as possible, to improve the representativeness of your sample. Remember that you will need to include details of your overall response rate in your evaluation.

Primary data: interviews

Interviews, both structured and unstructured, have certain advantages over questionnaires, although they are more difficult to analyse. Note, however, that the more standardised the interview, the easier it is to compare and quantify the results.

Interviews can allow the interviewer to follow-up respondents' replies, to explore motives and feelings and to gain additional information from the respondents' body language and tone of voice. This sensitivity to the interviewees' responses, including the ability to take note of what is not said as well as what is, is sometimes referred to as 'listening with the third ear'.

However, it should be borne in mind that as well as being difficult to analyse, interviews are very time-consuming, particularly unstructured ones, and the write-ups are inevitably highly subjective. Nevertheless, for some topic areas, interviews, either as the sole method or used in conjunction with other methods, are the most appropriate research tool, and provide rich sources of data.

As it is almost certain that, as a coursework student, you are an inexperienced interviewer, it is best to avoid completely unstructured interviews. You must decide whether your research topic best lends itself to a wholly structured or semi-structured approach. Both of these types of interview will require you to devise an 'interview schedule'. The schedule for a structured interview will look similar to a questionnaire, but will probably contain a higher proportion of open-ended questions. A semi-structured interview schedule will often consist of a series of topic headings, each to be introduced with a question, and each with a list of subsidiary points, which can be ticked off as the respondent covers them in the course of the response. Any areas left unticked can be covered by means of 'prompt' questions before going on to the next topic.

Research in Practice

Rachel's research project was an investigation into how the lives of women in Britain had changed over the last 60 years. She had decided to explore this after watching the television series Out of the Doll's House in her sociology class. With the help of the manager in charge of a local residential home for the elderly, Rachel had a group of five elderly ladies, all in their eighties, who had agreed to be interviewed.

Rachel was using semi-structured interviews, and her respondents had each agreed to be taped. She had carried out a practice interview with her grandmother, even though she was not in the right age group, to practise asking the questions and using the tape recorder, and to get an idea of how long each interview would last.

Rachel had identified a list of aspects of the women's lives that she wanted to gain information about, to make a comparison with young women of today. She knew that all of her respondents had been married, although they were now widowed.

Below is an extract from Rachel's interview schedule, showing the main topic areas she was going to cover, with a list of her subsidiary points for one area.

Main topic areas

- Childhood
- Schooling
- Work
- Courtship and marriage
- Child rearing (if applicable)
- Housework
- Neighbourhood/community life
- Decision-making in the home
- Opinions on women's lives today

Work

'I'd like you to tell me about what you did when you left school – did you go out to work? What kind of job did you do?'

Continued

Issues to be covered (tick when respondent deals with issue; prompt if not covered by end of this section):

- What kind of work?
- What were the (i) hours; (ii) rates of pay?
- How did she find out about the job?
- Were any qualifications required?
- Did she enjoy it? Why/why not?
- Did she carry on working when she got married?
- If yes, did she carry on working when she had children?

With interview schedules as with questionnaires, you should take time to get your questions/topic areas into the best order, so that there is an easy 'flow' to the interview.

9.1 Preparing for the interview

Interviews can take quite a long time to set up. Remember, the respondents are giving up their time for you, so you must be prepared, as far as possible, to fit in with their schedule.

Never conduct an interview without having practised asking the questions. If possible, tape your interviews (though you must obtain the respondent's permission to do this), and make absolutely sure that you know how to operate the recorder. Record your practice interview, and find out what the right volume setting is. Check the batteries (and carry a spare set just in case) or, if you are going to plug the machine into the mains, take an extension lead with you, to avoid your respondent having to be interviewed squashed into a corner with the recorder balanced precariously on top of the television!

When you set up the interview, indicate how long it will take and try to ensure that you will be able to conduct your interview undisturbed.

Research in Practice

Zoë was researching the issue of the problems encountered by working mothers. Part of her research involved finding out what was the situation locally. Below is a copy of her letter to the personnel officers of two of the largest local employers. This was sent out, with her teacher's approval, typed on her college headed notepaper.

Dear Ms Martin

I am a second-year A Level sociology student. As part of my course, I am carrying out a research project which is worth 15 per cent of my A Level mark.

I have decided to test the hypothesis that one of the reasons why some mothers with young children find it difficult to return to paid employment is the lack of 'family friendly' employment policies. I will be conducting interviews with a sample of mothers, and I would also like to find out about the employment policies of two major local employers, and the extent to which they have policies which would make it easier for mothers with young children to take a job with them.

I would be most grateful if you or a member of your department would agree to be interviewed about this. I anticipate that the interview would take between 20–30 minutes. I will, of course, travel to your premises and, with your permission, would also like to tape the interview, to help me write up the main points afterwards. Although my sociology teacher will know the name of your company, when I write up the research it will simply be identified as 'Company X'.

I look forward to hearing from you, and hope very much that you will be able to help me. I enclose a stamped, addressed envelope for your reply.

Yours sincerely

Zoë Webster

Think about your appearance, as the interviewee will be picking up clues about you, even unconsciously, and responding to them. As far as possible, you want to 'blend into the background' so that the interviewee talks freely and is not distracted by anything about you. Remember that your voice will be picked up on tape as well, so avoid jangly accessories. Tape your practice interview, so that you can check whether you have a nervous cough or giggle, or a tendency to talk too softly or too quickly.

9.2 During the interview

Make sure that you arrive on time, with all your notes and your recording equipment ready. Spend a few minutes putting the interviewee at ease, perhaps telling them a little about yourself and your course, especially if they are unknown to you. It is always worthwhile doing a 'sound check' before you start the interview if it is being taped. Remind the interviewee about the confidentiality of the conversation, and stress that, in your write-up, they will remain anonymous. Try to avoid making promises to show them your finished project, unless you are certain that you can and will do this.

Above all else, stick to the time. It is up to you to bring the interview to an end when you reach the agreed time. This is particularly important if you are interviewing someone at work. Even if you are carrying out the interview in someone's home, don't carry on recording for longer than you said. If the interviewee seems very keen to chat, and if you have the time to do so, then save this until the interview is finished and the recorder switched off. You do not want more data to analyse than you had planned for.

At the end of the interview, always remember to thank your respondent for their time. If you are interviewing someone from an outside organisation, it is also a good idea to write a brief letter of thanks as soon as possible afterwards. As well as being courteous, you are making it more likely that they will respond favourably to the next student who asks for an interview!

9.3 Writing up the interview

While taped interviews are extremely useful for checking responses, and also save you having to try to scribble everything down during the interview itself, they are very time-consuming to write up (transcribe). It has been calculated that every hour of recording takes, on average, ten hours to transcribe. Think carefully about this when deciding how many interviews to carry out, especially if they are semi-structured.

Give careful thought to how you will present the data generated by your interviews. You may be able to present some quantitative data, but much of your information will consist of your description and interpretation of the respondents' views. Where possible, and where relevant, try to include some direct quotations from the transcripts, i.e. using the interviewee's exact words. Such a technique is helpful to illustrate one person's expression of a view held by all or several of the respondents, or to show a selection of the different views on the same topic. It is also interesting to record a particularly appropriate or revealing turn of phrase used by a respondent.

Research in Practice

Khanh had applied to go to university and, if successful, would be the first member of his family to do so. However, he was increasingly concerned about the financial implications, for himself and also for his parents, who were working class, and who had very limited means at their disposal. In his study of the education topic, he had been reading about the expansion of higher education, and the increase in the number of working-class students at university, even if, as a proportion of the whole group, it was still small.

Khanh decided to explore the extent of financial pressures on university students, and the ways in which they coped with these. He had read in the newspapers about the number of students having to take part-time jobs to make ends meet, and was concerned about whether this particular education policy might have had an adverse effect on working-class applicants. He decided to take a case-study approach, based on a group of first-year undergraduates who had left his school Sixth Form that summer, and who would soon be home after their first term at university. He realised that this would be very early in their university career, but this was the group to which he had the easiest access, and he hoped that they would be able to give him information about other students from other years. Khanh knew that he had a very short time-scale to conduct his interviews; they would only be home for a couple of weeks and would have a number of social obligations, and possibly holiday jobs.

Continued

He knew that most of them would be back at school just before Christmas for the annual prize giving. Although he knew some of them, he realised that he might not get time to speak to them all, so he prepared a letter introducing himself, explaining the purpose of his research, and asking them to contact him to set up a convenient time for an interview. He thought that he could not reasonably expect anyone to spare him more than an hour. He prepared the letters, and drew up an interview schedule to make sure that all the areas of importance to him were covered.

Khanh also decided to try to arrange an interview with an admissions tutor at the local university, to see whether he could get a different perspective on the issue.

Coursework exercise

1   Draft a suitable *letter* which Khanh could hand to the students at the prize giving.

2   Draw up a list of *topic areas* which Khanh could use to help him construct his interview schedule.

3   Suggest a *practical* reason why Khanh might not be able to organise an interview with a university admissions tutor.

4   Suggest reasons why admissions tutors might not *wish* to discuss the issues raised by Khanh's research.

Primary data: observation

Observation as a research process is a highly-skilled activity. Generally speaking, for coursework purposes, covert participant observation is best avoided, not least because of ethical considerations. There are also practical problems, particularly for the inexperienced participant observer operating in a familiar situation, where certain activities which would prove very significant to an 'outsider' would often pass unnoticed due to their extreme 'everyday' familiarity.

For coursework students, the most manageable observation technique is usually structured observation. However, while it has the potential to yield a great deal of interesting data, this method will only work if it is carefully planned beforehand. Piloting the method is absolutely essential, so it is important not to leave the data collection to the last minute.

10.1 Deciding what to observe

This is the first and most important thing to decide as in any setting with which you are likely to be involved there will be so much happening that you can't possibly expect to record everything. You will need to be very specific about the categories of your observation, and not have too many of them.

10.2 The setting

Perhaps the most straightforward setting would be a classroom, but others might include the school/college common room, a children's playgroup, a supermarket, a courtroom or even a bus-stop.

Suppose that you were going to carry out observation in a classroom. The first thing, of course, is to obtain the permission of the teacher(s) concerned, and explain both the purpose of your research and how you are going to go about it. You will also find it helpful to make a plan of the classroom, so that you can indicate where, for example, male and female pupils sit, and where the teacher is in relation to the rest of the room. You should, of course, do this in advance of your observations, so that the plan is already drawn up ready to be filled in. You should also discuss with the teacher where you are going to sit while you make your observations. This will usually be at the back or at the side, as you don't want to be too obtrusive.

10.3 Planning the observation

Once you have drawn up your checklist of events to observe, these are the only ones you will be recording on your chart, so it is important to think carefully about your different categories. Pilot your observation chart over a couple of sessions, to see how easy it is to operate. Many students fall into the trap of including too many different categories of activity, and find that they can't keep up with recording the frequency of the different events.

Research in Practice

Surinder hoped to train as a social worker, and had a work-experience placement one afternoon a week at a local children's playgroup. She was studying A Level psychology as well as sociology, and was particularly interested in the nature/nurture debate with regard to gender differences, especially some of the feminist views.

She decided to carry out a structured observation study at the playgroup to see whether there was any noticeable gender difference in the kind of toys chosen by the boys and the girls, and also in the ways that they played with them. Surinder decided to draw up a grid which would enable her to note down quickly the kind of toy chosen by a child, the child's sex, and the kind of activity the toy was used for. She also decided to see whether the boys seemed more aggressive and assertive than the girls. She realised, of course, that not having access to the toys the children had at home, and how they were treated by their parents, meant that she would be unable to draw any conclusions about nature versus nurture, but she was still very interested in the general area.

She decided that she would also interview two of the full-time members of staff, using an unstructured interview, to see what their views were. She thought that, if she had time, she would also look carefully at press and television

Continued

advertisements for children's toys, to see whether these seemed to identify particular types of toy or game with a particular sex.

PLAYGROUP OBSERVATION

Date of observation: 2 February

Number of boys in the group: 9

No. of girls in the group: 13

Type of toy chosen	Number of incidences	
	Boys	Girls
Chooses construction-type toy (other than bricks)		
Chooses soft furry toy		
Chooses doll		
Chooses toy gun		
Chooses car/fire engine/ train/tractor		
Chooses book		
Chooses 'domestic' toy, e.g. vacuum cleaner, stove, dolls pram		
Chooses building bricks		
Chooses modelling clay		
Chooses dressing-up clothes		
Sitting/playing quietly		
Running around/shouting		
Building/making something		

Coursework exercise

1   Suggest an overall *aim* for Surinder's research.

2   Suggest possible *problems* with Surinder's observation grid.

3   Surinder wanted to see whether boys were 'more aggressive and assertive' than girls. Suggest why she might find it difficult to *operationalise* these characteristics.

10.4 Carrying out the observation

Make sure that you arrive early so that your entrance doesn't disrupt normal procedures. It is a good idea, in the classroom example, to wait until the class has settled and the lesson proper has begun, unless the preliminary activities could fall within your categories. Sit quietly and try to avoid eye-contact with those whom you are observing, some of whom, especially if they are school pupils, might be only too willing to put on a special performance for you!

At the end of the session, remember to thank the teacher/organiser, but try to avoid getting drawn into a detailed discussion regarding what you have just observed.

10.5 Writing up the observations

Structured observations lend themselves to an interesting blend of quantitative and qualitative data. While your observation charts and room plans will give you some numerical data, you will also need to describe, interpret and analyse the observed behaviours. Make sure that any conclusions you draw are supported by your numerical data, even if these refute your original hypothesis.

10.6 The research diary in progress

The following pages provide you with an extract from a student's research diary partway through the research process. Read it carefully, to note how the student is jotting down ideas and working through some unexpected problems. There is also a coursework exercise based on these entries on page 80.

Table 10.1 An example of the later entries of a research diary

Research diary for sociology coursework

Title: Gender and subject choice in science

Date	Ideas	Problems	Possible solutions	Sources	Comments	Coursework section
Sept 14	Need to choose method. I like the idea of interviews.	Might not be able to get enough data from interviews.	1 Use structured interviews. 2 Use questionnaires	Pros/cons of different methods in class notes and text book.	Questionnaires would give me a lot more data – more reliable?	Methodology
	Probably a good idea to have some national statistical data for comparison.	Not sure where to get hold of this.	Ask librarian for help.	Librarian recommended *Social Trends*.	Found what I wanted in *Social Trends*.	
Sept 23	Will take a sample of pupils to fill in questionnaire.	What is best method? One of my population groups is in another school!	Will use random sampling. Will put pile of questionnaires in my school dining room and send batch to Newtown Comprehensive and ask Head of Year 11 to distribute for me.	Read text book and class notes on sampling. Note advantages of different sampling techniques to inform evaluation section.	Met with teacher (Sept 30) who pointed out some problems with my sampling method, mainly complete lack of control over who fills them in. Decided to draw random sample of 75 Year	Methodology Content Evaluation

Table 10.1 continued

Date	Ideas	Problems	Possible solutions	Sources	Comments	Coursework section
					11 girls in my school (every pupil has a roll number) and issue to named pupils. Will take 120 questionnaires to Newtown school and ask Head of Year 11 to give them to 5 boys and 5 girls in each Year 11 class (12 classes in all), taking the 2,4,7,10 and 13th boy and girl in each class register.	
Oct 14	Need to write questionnaire	Not sure how many questions to have and whether they should be closed or open-ended.	Write a questionnaire and pilot it.	Read class notes and relevant section in A–Z coursework book	Wrote questionnaire and piloted it on some Year 11 girls in my drama group	Content

A B C D E F G H I J K L M N O P Q R S T U V W X Y Z

Table 10.1 continued

Date	Ideas	Problems	Possible solutions	Sources	Comments	Coursework section
Oct 21	Re: pilot	Some questions didn't seem to be clear to pilot group. Also, a few girls wanted to know why I needed their father's occupation, and one girl said her father hadn't been around since she was 2 and she hadn't got the faintest idea what job he did.	Re-draft questionnaire.		Met with teacher to show her revised questionnaire. She agreed that I didn't need to know father's occupation, as not considering social class as a variable. One or two questions still ambiguous or misleading. Teacher told me to refer to A–Z coursework book for help in writing questions.	Methodology Content Evaluation
Nov 9		Went to collect questionnaires from Newtown Comprehensive. Found out that 10	1 Do Newtown questionnaires again – not enough time? Would they still be willing to		Will accept Newtown questionnaires (94 completed, but several 'joke'	Methodology Content Evaluation

Table 10.1 continued

Date	Ideas	Problems	Possible solutions	Sources	Comments	Coursework section
		questionnaires placed in each Year 11 register, but then just handed out to anybody willing to take one.	help me? 2 Leave Newtown out of sample – but then no boys for comparison!		ones that I must throw away). Must remember that no longer a proper random sample, as only interested pupils took them.	
		Very low response rate from my school. Found several questionnaires still in class registers – not even handed out! Many given out still not returned.	Cross students who have completed Qs off my list. Get permission to get rest of sample together one break time (provide free hot drinks and biscuits!) and get them to fill in Q there and then.		Got permission – it worked very well. Nearly everybody turned up and filled in questionnaire.	
Nov 11	Need to analyse data	Don't know where to begin! 157 completed questionnaires!	Make a grid to record information (wish I'd done this at the beginning!)	Check A–Z coursework book.	Grid working well but very time-consuming. Wish I'd tried to analyse pilot Qs	Methodology Content

A B C D E F G H I J K L M N O P Q R S T U V W X Y Z

Table 10.1 continued

Date	Ideas	Problems	Possible solutions	Sources	Comments	Coursework section
					instead of just reading them. Think I've asked too many questions.	
Nov 20	Present as much data as possible in tabular/graphical format.	Not very good at using computer to draw bar-charts/pie charts.	1 See IT teacher for help. 2 Get help from nerdy 6th former always playing on computer.	See if anything in Resource Centre which would help.	IT teacher has no extra time to help me. Great! Can do it now. Great fun, really – not hard at all.	Content
Dec 6		Still struggling with all the data. Haven't dealt with half of it yet, and fast running out of time.	Sit down and decide what is REALLY SIGNIFICANT data in terms of my hypothesis. Do in-depth comment and analysis on this, with much briefer comments on other bits. Leave some info out altogether.	Examples of good coursework sent by exam board for reference. Check studies to see how sociologists select, present and analyse data.	Met with teacher who agreed with me on what data to focus on. This seems to be working. Feel more in control now. Will finish it over the Christmas holiday.	Content

11 The evaluation and conclusions

Evaluative commentary should feature throughout your coursework. In the context and methodology sections of your project you have the opportunity to comment on the respective strengths and weaknesses of the secondary source material you use and the methods you consider. The final section of your research should provide the examiner with an overall evaluation of your research. This is also the section of your coursework where you summarise your findings in the form of a conclusion. It is also the place to make recommendations for future research and note any implications for social policy.

Many students think that for their research to be good they have to 'prove' their hypothesis. This is not true! Examiners are looking to reward rigorous research. It is important that you are honest about all the problems you experience when conducting your research. The examiner is looking to see if you are sensitive to design flaws, recognise them and are able to offer possible solutions. The examiner wants to know about the practical problems you have encountered when using your method. All researchers have practical problems when carrying out their research, and you are no different. The purpose of research is not to prove or disprove theories but to collect evidence which provides a basis from which readers can make an informed judgement about an issue. You will gain marks for being critical of the way in which you conduct your research, so do not try to cover up any difficulties you experience, but always make a note in your research diary of the difficulties you have. Similarly, do not invent problems because you want to be seen to be critical. The examiner will see through this and you are more likely to present contradictory information which will undermine the quality of the rest of your research.

Some students think that it is important to say that everything went well, and either hide the problems they had or demonstrate insensitivity to problems as they emerge. The evaluation and conclusion section from such students is often self-congratulatory, and demonstrates very little ability to reflect critically on the research process. They therefore cannot get high marks.

To try to ensure a high mark for this section of the coursework it is sensible to devote a few weeks to planning and writing it, discussing it with others and then editing it into its finished form. You should study your research diary carefully, as it should have most of the information you need for the evaluation section of your project. Your research diary should be a record of the research journey with all its problems, solutions and additional comments. If you follow the advice on page 17 then you will have a research diary which notes problems and solutions for each stage of the research. This will be very helpful if you adopt the structure outlined on page 75 when writing your evaluation of the research process.

Both AQA and OCR students should provide:

- **an evaluation of, and justification for, the overall research design and methodology employed**

- **an assessment of research findings with reference to the issues raised in the rationale and recommendations for further research.**

Research in Practice

Leroy's elder brother was in his second year of training to be a nurse. Leroy was interested by his brother's accounts of how different patients reacted to being treated by a male nurse, and also by some of the reactions he himself got when he told people that his brother was a nurse. Leroy decided that he would explore the topic of gendered occupations, and try to find out whether the reasons for young men entering the nursing profession and their experiences within it were in any way different from those of young women, as well as exploring the issue of stereotypes. His brother broached the topic with some of his fellow trainees, and a dozen of them, including two other males, agreed to be interviewed. Leroy was a little unsure of what questions he should ask, so decided to carry out a pilot interview with his brother and a female nurse before interviewing the other nurses. He also thought that he would conduct a survey among his own classmates at college, to see whether they had any preferences for being treated by male or female nurses, and if so, the reasons for these.

Coursework exercise

1   Suggest a suitable *source* for Leroy to find further information on 'gendered occupations'.

2   Write three questions which you think that Leroy should include in his *pilot interview*, stating your reasons for their inclusion.

11.1 How to structure your evaluation section

There are many different ways of structuring your evaluation and conclusion section. You should select the one which best suits your research and preferred way of writing. Whichever structure you use, it is important that you provide the examiner with a rigorous assessment of your research journey. This should address the extent to which you successfully or otherwise delivered the tasks you set in the rationale. Remember the question the examiner is continually asking as she/he reads your coursework is: 'Has this student researched what s/he said they would?'.

The rationale is the theme which runs through the entire coursework. In your evaluation section you should return to the hypothesis/aims and objectives you set yourself, and assess the extent to which these were addressed and delivered.

One way of structuring your evaluation and conclusion section is to reflect on each stage of your research journey. To do this, you take each section of your report and comment on the strengths and weaknesses of that section. A useful way to do this is to assess the extent to which the activities you undertook for that section helped you or impeded you in realising your research hypothesis/aim and objectives.

Thus in your critical reflection of the rationale, you may find it appropriate to comment on some of the following:

*   **the extent to which your hypothesis/aim/objectives proved to be clear, researchable and relevant**

*   **the extent to which you needed to refine, reduce or even change your hypothesis/aim and objectives during the research period, and the reasons for this**

*   **the usefulness of the sociological concepts and theories identified in the rationale in developing your research focus**

*   **the extent to which your preliminary observations and values influenced your research practice**

- **the themes from your rationale which were followed through in your research.**

In your assessment of the context section you may find it appropriate to comment on some of the following:

- **the area(s) of the syllabus from which your research emerges**

- **any theoretical preference you may have, your reasons for such a preference, and how this may have influenced your research**

- **the extent to which your findings reflect or challenge established research in the field, noting any reasons for the differences**

- **the socio-political context of any secondary research or official statistics you have used, and any implications of this for your research**

- **key concepts used (e.g. class, religiosity, power) and how successful you were in operationalising them.**

When evaluating your research design and the methodology you employed, you should comment on some of the following:

- **theoretical issues and reasons for your choice of research design and methodology**

- **practical reasons for your choice of methodology (e.g. time, resources)**

- **justification for your chosen methodology in the light of the tasks you set in the rationale**

- **any practical problems you experienced in employing your methodology (e.g. problems with the organisations or individuals you contacted, or difficulties with participants/respondents), and how you responded to these problems**

- **any difficulties you had with operationalising key concepts (e.g. religiosity, class, power) and the strategies you used, or would use in the future, to overcome these difficulties**

- **any problems arising from sampling (e.g. the suitability of any sampling frame used, and the method of sampling chosen), and how you dealt with these**

- **the efforts you made to meet the BSA ethical guidelines**

- an evaluation of your data collection in terms of its validity, reliability, representativeness, generalisability, objectivity, subjectivity, triangulation, etc.

- the usefulness of the pilot questionnaire, interview schedule, observation process you devised

- any other problems you experienced and the effectiveness of strategies used to resolve them.

In addition, if appropriate, you should:

- offer alternative methods for your research

- suggest further refinements to your methodology which could improve the quality of further research.

When writing the conclusion section of your research you should:

- summarise clearly the overall findings of your research

- link these findings to each hypothesis, aim and objective you set in the rationale

- demonstrate sociological insight in the way you interpret your findings

- offer recommendations for further development of your research

- note any implications for social policy.

11.2 Research based on secondary sources

Students whose research is based exclusively on secondary source material must also provide an evaluation and conclusion section. Much of the advice on evaluating the rationale and context given on pages 75–76 applies to research based on secondary sources. However the evaluation of the methodology for secondary based research should:

- assess the research design and methodology of the secondary source(s) used

- assess the advantages and disadvantages of using secondary source material for delivering the hypothesis/aim and objectives stated in the rationale

- address issues of validity, reliability, representativeness, objectivity, subjectivity as they relate to the source material(s) used

* **discuss the implications of the theoretical framework of the secondary source material employed.**

Research in Practice

Carolyn was taking A levels in Sociology, Art and English literature. She was studying the Victorian period in both Art and English, and decided that she would like to do a comparative study of the portrayal of family life in both Victorian art and literature, informed by sociological insight and using a range of relevant sociological concepts drawn from her study of the sociology of the family.

She discussed the idea with her teachers in all three subjects. Her art and English teachers thought it an excellent idea, but her sociology teacher was more cautious in her response, and advised Carolyn to think carefully about the breadth of what she was proposing to do. Carolyn was asked to go away and draw up a working title, a suitable hypothesis or aim, and a list of objectives, as well as identifying the major sources she would use.

When Carolyn started to do this, she quickly became aware of what a huge task she had set herself, and realised that her original idea would need to be modified to make it more manageable. She talked again to her art teacher, and looked through some of the books in the art department library, and then decided that she would narrow her focus to look at the portrayal of childhood in Victorian painting, using the sociological idea of childhood as a social construct.

At the next meeting with her sociology teacher, Carolyn put forward her revised proposal. She explained that her art teacher had already directed her towards some books on Victorian art which explained the use of symbolism in this period, and Carolyn had decided that she would also do some research into the reality of Victorian childhood. She already knew something about the extent of poverty and the widespread use of child labour at this time.

The A level art group was soon to go on a visit to two major art galleries in London, so Carolyn knew that she

Continued

would be able to study some suitable examples. She also intended to talk to the curator of the local museum, which had an art gallery with several examples of Victorian paintings by local artists.

Carolyn's teacher approved her new idea, but said that Carolyn must make absolutely sure that her focus was a sociological one.

Coursework exercise

1 **Suggest a sociological text which would prove useful to Carolyn.**

2 **From your own knowledge and the information above, make a list of a sociological concepts which Carolyn could use in her research.**

The dos and don'ts of an evaluation

Project dos	Project don'ts

Project dos

☑ Leave yourself at least two weeks to plan and write your evaluation.

☑ Justify your methodology with reference to the hypothesis, aim, objectives you set.

☑ Provide details of all problems.

☑ Discuss how validity, reliability, representativeness relate to your research.

☑ Comment on similarities/ differences between your findings and the sociological research you cite in your context section.

☑ Provide recommendations for improving your methodology.

☑ Provide a conclusion.

Project don'ts

☒ Do your evaluation the night before your deadline for handing in your coursework.

☒ List all the advantages of each method you use.

☒ Hide or make up problems.

☒ Explore terms which are not relevant to your methodology.

☒ Provide detailed accounts of similar research done by other sociologists.

☒ Be self-congratulatory and say everything went well and to plan.

☒ Mix your conclusion in with your evaluation.

Coursework exercise

Refer back to the example of a research diary on pages 68–72.

1   **Identify one *problem* experienced by this student, and offer a critical *evaluation* of the proposed solution(s).**

2   **Suggest an *alternative* research method for this topic, giving reasons for your answer.**

Checklist 4

Have I completed my evaluation?

Completed

Yes No

1 Have I offered justification for the method(s) used? ☐ ☐

2 Have I addressed issues of reliability, validity, representativeness, bias, etc.? ☐ ☐

3 Have I linked the research findings to the hypothesis/aim? ☐ ☐

4 Have I addressed all the objectives in the rationale, OR given explanations for any changes? ☐ ☐

5 Have I identified any practical/ethical problems encountered and explained what steps were taken to try to overcome these? ☐ ☐

6 Have I suggested alternative methods which might have been used? ☐ ☐

7 Have I made recommendations for the further development of the research? ☐ ☐

8 Have I provided a conclusion which clearly summarises the overall findings of the research? ☐ ☐

A B C D E F G H I J K L M N O P Q R S T U V W X Y Z

Presentation

You will find a great deal of help regarding the use of information technology to present your work in Chapter 17. In addition, these few simple rules will help to ensure that your work is presented in the best possible way.

1   **If at all possible, word-process your project. Not only does this make it easier to read, but it enables you to take advantage of other useful features, such as the ability to cut-and-paste, to use underlining, bold type and italics to emphasise points, to insert graphics, to have automatic page-numbering, to do a word-count and to use the spell-check facility. If you really have to write out your project by hand, do so as neatly as possible, write on one side of the paper only, and write your page numbers initially in pencil until you are sure of the right order.**

2   **If your project is word-processed, use double spacing throughout.**

3   **It is rare for a project to need no revisions, so you must be prepared to draft and re-draft until you are satisfied with the result. Check your grammar and punctuation, and ensure that you have not used inappropriate language, such as that which is sexist or racist. Remember that, while spell-checkers are very useful, they are not fool-proof, so you will need to do a manual check, looking for the incorrect application of words such as there/their, its/it's, whether/weather, to/two/too, personal/personnel, principle/principal, etc.**

4   **Start each section on a fresh page, following the order required by your particular awarding body.**

5   **When using graphics, choose the most appropriate way of presenting your data. It is most important that you do not let the information in your tables or graphics 'speak for itself'. Every table, graph, bar chart, pie chart or other graphic must be clearly labelled as Figure 1, Table 3.2, etc. so that you can refer to it in the text, e.g. 'As Figure 1 shows ...' Each graphic must also have a title, which shows clearly what the information represents. In addition, every table or graphic should be accompanied by a brief comment which points out its significance to**

your research and, where possible, relates it to other relevant information, as in Table 12.1 below.

Table 12.1 GCSE achievements: by gender and selected subject 1994–95

Subject	Percentage achieving grades C and above	
	Males	**Females**
Science double award	49	50
Science single award	38	44
Biological science	81	78
Chemistry	85	86
Physics	87	88
Other science	34	33

Source: *Social Trends* Volume 27, 1997

Example of a suitable comment on Table 12.1

Table 12.1 is interesting as it shows that, contrary to what is often thought, girls generally do as well as, and in some cases better than, boys at GCSE science. Even in physics, in which girls are under-represented at A level, the proportion of girls achieving grade C or above is marginally higher than that of boys. This would seem to show that, if many girls do not take physics and chemistry at A Level, it is not because they can't, or think that they can't, perform well in these subjects.

Example of a suitable comment on Figure 12.1

Figure 12.1 shows the percentage of A Level students choosing science subjects in the two different schools looked at. School X is the all-female grant-maintained school, while School Y is the mixed-sex comprehensive school.

The bar chart shows that a higher proportion of girls in School X take A Level science than in School Y. Indeed, a higher proportion of girls in School X take science than boys at School Y, although the difference is not very great in chemistry and physics, and is most marked in biology.

The similarity between the percentages of School X females and School Y males studying physics and chemistry at A Level would appear to cast some

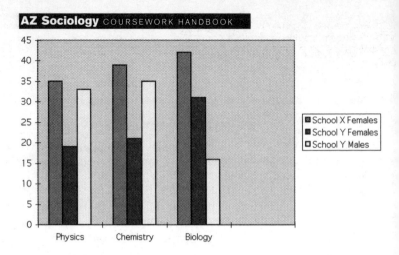

Figure 12.1 Science subject choice at A Level by gender

doubt on the findings of Castleman and Poole (1990), who show that there is still important gender segregation in subject choice, especially at university. However, it is important to note that School X is an all-female establishment with a strong tradition of A Level science, and also that the proportion of girls taking physics or chemistry at School Y is much lower than that of boys.

Nevertheless, my findings could be argued to indicate that the growing success of girls in science at GCSE since it has become a national curriculum subject is leading to a higher proportion of females taking A Levels in science than in the past.

AQA A2 coursework

AQA sociology coursework has several distinctive features, each of which is explained fully in this book.

The features include:

- **a choice between doing primary or secondary based research**
- **a maximum target length of 3500 words with suggested word lengths for the different sections**
- **fully explained marking criteria**
- **internal assessment and external moderation.**

13.1 Demonstrating the skills

A2 coursework provides you with the opportunity to demonstrate all the skills covered by assessment objectives 1 and 2. Below is some guidance showing how you can ensure good coverage of the required skills.

Skill area	Ways of demonstrating skill
Knowledge and understanding	<ul><li>provide the reader with a clear explanation of key theories and concepts used</li><li>provide accurate details of the secondary research to which reference is made</li><li>give a brief and accurate summary of your context material</li><li>show a thorough and detailed understanding of all aspects of your chosen method, particularly as it relates to your hypothesis/aim</li><li>organise your material in a clear, logical and coherent manner</li></ul>

Skill area	Ways of demonstrating skill
Identification and interpretation	• identify appropriate research studies which help to contextualise your research focus • where appropriate, identify historical and cross-cultural data to contextualise your research • show the ways in which the material you use relates to sociological theories • where appropriate, use statistical data to inform and interpret trends in the secondary sources you have used • use sociological insight to interpret the data you have collected
Analysis and evaluation	• use a critical approach to all material throughout, including sociological theories and concepts, the secondary material you have used and any data you collect yourself • comment on any biases in secondary sources used, and the resulting implications for the research conclusions (e.g. theoretical, political, cultural) • examine critically the reliability and validity of the methodology used in your secondary sources, including your context material • examine critically any shortcomings in your own method of data collection

13.2 Target word length

The rules of the AQA coursework are clear in that they strongly recommend that the project does not exceed 3500 words.

At the outset, most students find it hard to think how they will write as many as 3500 words. Towards the end, it is not uncommon for some students to find that their project is over 4000 words long, so it is important to keep a check on the length.

To help you do this, the AQA provides you with suggested ranges for each of the sections. Note that these are suggestions only and you may wish to organise your research folder differently. The suggested ranges are as follows:

- **Rationale:**   250–300 words
- **Context:**   750–850 words
- **Methodology:**   550–650 words
- **Evidence:**   950–1050 words
- **Evaluation:**   700–800 words

The reality is that examiners are unlikely to count your words. It is, however, very unlikely that the extra words will gain you extra marks. In fact, as well as taking up too much time, such an approach often leads to a loss of focus.

So how do you make sure you produce a good project which meets all the skills, achieves the appropriate depth and keeps within the recommended word length? There are three key points to remember.

1 Set clear objectives from the start
   Many projects wander because students start without clearly defined and achievable objectives.

2 Be sure to include only that information which is relevant to your project
   For example the context section should summarise only those studies which provide the essential context which provides the reader with a framework for understanding the focus and purpose of your research. Similarly the methodology section should focus only on the method which you intend to use in your research. You do not need to discuss the advantages and disadvantages of every sociological method.

3 Edit your work thoroughly
   It is rare for anyone to achieve a good product at the first attempt. You will need to re-read your work constantly and remove any material which is repeated elsewhere, or digresses from the focus and objectives you established in the rationale. You will find this editing process much easier if your work has been word-processed and saved on disk.

13.3 The AQA A2 marking criteria

It is always important to know how a piece of work is to be marked. What are the key criteria for success? Make sure that you are familiar with the details of the mark scheme, which you will find in the specification.

In line with questions in all the other units, the coursework is marked out of 60. There are two separate mark schemes from which to choose, depending on whether the main research method involves the gathering of primary data, or the use of secondary data. Whichever mark scheme is used, the mark allocations and the weighting of the assessment objectives are the same.

The 60 available marks are divided between the two assessment objectives as shown below:

AO1

    Knowledge and understanding   24 marks

AO2

    Identification, analysis, interpretation and evaluation   36 marks

The 60 available marks are also divided between the different sections of the coursework, as shown in the table below.

Remember also that quality of communication is assessed throughout your project. This does not mean simply using correct spelling and punctuation, but also being able to express your ideas in a clear and logical manner, using relevant sociological concepts correctly.

Assessment objective	Section of coursework	Marks
AO1 Knowledge and understanding	• Context	12
	• Methodology	12
AO2 Identification, analysis, interpretation and evaluation	• Application, presentation, interpretation and analysis of method(s) and data	18
	• Rationale, evaluation and conclusions	18

13.4 Internally assessed but externally moderated

Your project will initially be marked by your teacher. If there is more than one sociology teacher in your school or college, every teacher should mark some projects from each class and arrive at an agreed mark. This important process is called standardisation. As it takes time to do this thoroughly it is particularly important that you hand in your project on the date you have been given.

When all the projects have been marked, a sample chosen by AQA has to be sent to an external moderator. This is someone who marks the projects again to ensure that the AQA standard has been applied.

13.5 Writing up the project

Use the structure recommended by AQA, that is:

- **title page (include your full name , centre name and number and candidate number)**
- **candidate record form (your teacher will tell you about this)**
- **contents page (list of the main headings and their page numbers)**
- **rationale**
- **context**
- **methodology**
- **evidence (data collected and analysed)**
- **evaluation.**

You should then include the following:

- **bibliography (an alphabetical list of all the sources used)**
- **a photocopied extract of one page of your research diary showing research in progress.**
- **appendices – include any of the following which are relevant: one example of a pilot questionnaire/interview schedule, and a copy of the final document; a copy of each letter sent and received (with logos/names/addresses removed).**

Other points to note:

- **start each section on a new page**
- **number every page**
- **use treasury tags rather than a hard folder to keep your work together.**

A
B
C
D
E
F
G
H
I
J
K
L
M
N
O
P
Q
R
S
T
U
V
W
X
Y
Z

14 The OCR A2 personal study

The OCR personal study is an extended piece of work on a sociological topic chosen by the student. The task for students, as set out in the OCR specification, is as follows:

- **to design a sociological investigation using primary and/or secondary data**

- **to try out this design by assembling a limited, but illustrative amount of data**

- **to demonstrate the ability to identify facts, opinions and value judgements**

- **to evaluate the outcome of the exercise in terms of the strengths and weaknesses of the research design and of any data collected**

- **to demonstrate the ability to relate their knowledge of sociological theory and methods to their research experience.**

14.1 Target word length

OCR state that the 'main content' of the personal study should be between 2000 and 2500 words. The 'main content' refers to the rationale section (500–750 words), the research section (750–1000 words) and the evaluation section (750–1000 words). The total word length of the personal study must be stated on the title page.

So how do you make sure that you produce a good piece of work which demonstrates all the skills, achieves the appropriate depth and keeps within the recommended word length? There are three key points to remember:

1 **Set clear objectives from the start**
   Many projects lose their focus because students start without clearly defined and achievable objectives.

2 **Include only information that is relevant to your study**
   For example, the rationale should focus only on those methods you

actually used in your research. You do not need to discuss the advantages and disadvantages of every sociological method.

3   **Edit your work thoroughly**
     It is rare for anyone to achieve a good product at the first attempt. You will need to re-read your work constantly and remove any material which is repeated elsewhere, or which digresses from the focus and objectives you established in your rationale. You will, of course, find this process much easier if your work has been wordprocessed and saved on disk.

14.2 The OCR marking criteria

It is always important to know how a piece of work is to be assessed, so make sure that you are familiar with the assessment matrix in the specification. The personal study is worth 15 per cent of the A level mark, divided between AO1 (7 per cent) and AO2 (8 per cent). It is marked out of 90, with 42 marks allocated for AO1 and 48 marks for AO2.

14.3 The research proposal

An outline of your proposed topic and research method(s) has to be submitted to OCR for approval before you start your personal study. Your teacher is allowed to offer guidance and support in helping you to choose an appropriate topic.

14.4 External assessment

The personal study is externally assessed, which means that it is sent by your teacher to OCR and marked by OCR examiners.

14.5 Writing up the personal study

You must use the structure recommended by OCR. Your personal study should have numbered pages and include the following sections:

1   **Title page** – showing the number of words.

2   **List of contents** – presented as a single separate page.

3   **Rationale** – which should include a statement of your research issue, question or hypothesis, a statement of your reasons for carrying out the

study and a description, explanation and justification of your research design and procedure.

4   **Research** – this should be organised under a number of suitable sub-headings.

5   **Evaluation** – this should include an evaluation of the overall research design and methodology, some assessment of your findings and any ideas for further development of the research.

6   **Bibliography** – this should include a list of the sources you used, including any Internet websites.

7   **Appendix** – this should include a copy of your proposal, one example of, for example, a questionnaire you have used, and one example of any letters of enquiry you sent and the answers you received.

8   **Research diary** – listing your progress chronologically, in notes made at the time.

9   **Annexe** – this is not submitted with your personal study, but must be kept carefully until you have your result. The annexe should contain all the material you gathered during the course of your research.

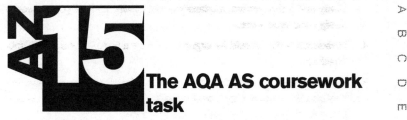

15 The AQA AS coursework task

The AQA AS coursework task has several distinct features. These include:

- **a class-based research design task which does not include undertaking primary research**
- **a choice of topic**
- **a maximum recommended word length**
- **a required structure, each part with its own recommended word length**
- **an opportunity to use the AS research proposal as the basis for the A2 coursework.**

15.1 How to use this section

This section gives you a great deal of information, help and advice regarding the AQA coursework task. You should read it through before starting on your research proposal. It is broken down into four sub-sections, each corresponding to one of the sections in which your coursework task has to be presented for marking.

Each of the sub-sections which follow contains a description and an example of a student's work, headed 'Research in Practice' together with some related tasks for you to do (called a 'Coursework Exercise'). You will probably find it most helpful to study the Research in Practice examples and do the Coursework Exercises section by section, as you reach that stage in your own research proposal. The ideal way of doing these exercises is with a friend, so that you can discuss your answers. You might even be able to discuss these with your teacher, especially those which ask you to suggest a mark band for the student's work. Remember, however, that your teacher is a very busy person, so don't automatically assume that there will be time available for this.

It is important that you obtain a copy of the mark scheme and study it thoroughly. By being able to identify and understand the requirements of the top band, you should be able to cast a critical eye over your own work and identify whether it falls short of these requirements and why.

15.2 The nature of the coursework task

Students choosing this option for AS Unit 3 are required to submit a research proposal which could form the basis of a piece of sociological research. An important point to remember is that the proposal submitted at AS may, if a student wishes, be used as the basis of A2 coursework. On the other hand, it doesn't need to. This means that if you want to, you can submit an AS research proposal for a piece of sociological research which could not realistically be carried out by a 17-year old school or college student. It might be that it would be too expensive, too time-consuming, or would need access to groups or data which would be impossible for an AS student to obtain. However, provided the submission meets all the required criteria, this is quite acceptable. On the other hand, if you think that there is a possibility that you might wish to develop your AS proposal into a piece of A2 coursework, you should make sure that the initial proposal is one which is realistic in terms of the time and resources which will be available to you in your second year of the course.

The research proposal has to be submitted under four given headings, and has a maximum word length of 1200 words. Each of the four sections has its own maximum word length, and it is most important that your proposal fall within the maximum word lengths given by AQA. As well as writing the total number of words on the cover, the number of words for each section should be given at the end of that section. That way, the markers can easily see whether or not you have been successful in meeting this particular goal.

15.3 The skills

The coursework task is worth 30 per cent of the total marks for the AS qualification, and for those students going on to A2, 15 per cent of the total A level qualification. Marks are awarded on the basis of two skill areas, or assessment objectives, known as AO1 and AO2, each worth half of the available marks. AO1 covers the skills of knowledge and understanding, and the effective communication of this knowledge and understanding. AO2 covers a variety of skills, namely identification, analysis, interpretation and evaluation. The task is marked out of 60, and each section has its own mark allocation, as shown below:

Section	Number of marks	Number of words
Hypothesis or aim	8	100
Context and concepts	20	400
Main research method and reasons	20	400
Potential problems	12	300
Total	60	1200

15.4 Choice of topic

The chosen topic must fall within the bounds of the specification. This includes both the substantive topics and the core themes. In practice it would be unwise to choose a research focus which falls outside those areas you have studied at the time you start your coursework task. This is because it is much more difficult for you to select appropriate pieces of context material and relevant concepts when you are unfamiliar with the area.

This limitation may mean that you are not the only person in your class to choose a particular area. This doesn't matter, provided that what you submit is entirely your own work. Remember, your teacher has to sign a form saying that, to the best of her/his knowledge, what you have done is your own work. This doesn't mean that you can't share ideas with your classmates, or even receive or pass on details of potentially suitable material. It does mean that everything you write is in your own words and genuinely reflects your own ideas.

15.5 Getting started

Before you even think of writing anything, you must familiarise yourself with the four section headings and the mark scheme. Together, these will help you to understand what you must do and what you must do to get good marks. You will probably go through several outline drafts, such as the one on the following page, before you proceed with the first draft of the whole proposal.

Research in Practice

Brendan's teacher had given everyone in the class an A4 sheet of paper headed with the four sections of the coursework task. The homework task was to make a first attempt at identifying what would go in each of the sections; later this would be discussed with the teacher. This is what Brendan prepared as the basis of that discussion.

Hypothesis/aim

Aim: to investigate a sample of white and Asian families in Leicester to see whether or not the extended family plays an important part in their lives.

Topic area: Families and households

Context and concepts

Context 1: P. Willmott 'Urban Kinship Past and Present' Sociology Review, November 1988.

Context 2: J. Finch and J. Mason 'Negotiating Family Responsibilities', 1993

Concept 1: dispersed extended family

Concept 2: social role

Main research method and reasons

Structured interviews with a sample of white and Asian families – probably about 20 in all. Sample not random but opportunistic – will use families of college friends from both communities, both working-class and middle-class. Will look at things like frequency of contact and whether this is face to face, by phone, e-mail, letter, etc. Will also look at geographical proximity of family members to each other. Will also ask about help given to or received from members of extended family, and what kind of help (e.g. financial, services like baby-sitting, helping when sick, etc.)

Reasons: too complex an area just to do by questionnaire; need more qualitative data to try to uncover 'importance' of extended family to different groups.

Continued

Potential problems

- sample probably not representative
- time to organise, carry out and analyse the interviews
- will need to ask Asian friend to come along to some interviews to act as translator, as some of the older family members will not speak good English.

Coursework exercise

Brendan's teacher was quite pleased with what he had done, but there were a few important issues to be considered before Brendan could make a start. Brendan made a note of these, and they are shown below. Look at each of them, and decide how Brendan might deal with them.

1 **The aim could be restated as a hypothesis. What might this be?**

2 **What was it about the topic area that interested me (be sociological!)**

3 **How will the concept of 'social role' be operationalised?**

4 **How will I decide on the 'importance' of the extended family? What criteria will I choose?**

5 **Note: if I chose to do this as my A2 research, I wouldn't be able to carry out and analyse 20 interviews. This doesn't matter – six would be quite acceptable.**

6 **Is it necessary to have 'class' as a variable as well as 'ethnicity', especially given the relatively small number of families involved?**

7 **Are there any potential ethical problems involved, given the likely nature of some of the questions? If so, what are these ethical problems?**

Now look again at Brendan's proposed concepts. Write a brief definition of each of these in the context of his chosen aim, that is, show how the definition is relevant to the chosen area of investigation.

15.6 Section 1: Hypothesis/aim

It is absolutely essential that you choose an appropriate hypothesis or aim; if you get this part wrong you will almost certainly run into difficulties with the remainder of the coursework task. So what is meant by 'appropriate'? Your hypothesis or aim should satisfy the following criteria:

- **It should come from part of the sociology specification – that is, from one of the topic areas or from one of the two core themes.**

- **It should have a *sociological focus* – that is, it should show clearly that you have been thinking like a sociologist when you identified both the general area and the particular hypothesis or aim.**

- **It should have a *specific focus* – a common mistake among students is to make the focus far too broad, which will lead to problems in the AS coursework task, and will make it almost impossible to use this as the basis for an A2 coursework project.**

- **It should enable the research issue to be progressed – that is, it should be possible to support it with appropriate pieces of context, should be possible to investigate it using an appropriate sociological method, and the data collected should lend themselves to analysis using relevant sociological concepts.**

- **It should be possible to track your hypothesis/aim throughout the research proposal – that is, there should be a clear link between each of the sections of the proposal back to the original hypothesis/aim.**

- **It should be a topic in which you are genuinely interested – this becomes even more important if it is carried over into the A2 coursework.**

Before you even think of starting the coursework task you should consider all of what you study in sociology in terms of its potential to generate an appropriate hypothesis or aim. Not only does this give you important practice in formulating hypotheses and aims, but it makes it more likely that when you do have to choose a particular focus, you will be able to do so more easily, as you will have been considering a range of different issues throughout the course.

It is vital, of course, that you understand the difference between a hypothesis and an aim. Put simply:

A hypothesis is a testable statement which assumes a particular situation or predicts an outcome. An example would be: 'Children from working-class backgrounds will generally have poorer educational qualifications than children from middle-class backgrounds.' This is stating something as a 'fact', and it is a statement which can be tested against empirical evidence, in this case, the relative qualifications of working-class and middle-class children. It is, of course, more complex than it seems at first glance – what do we mean by 'generally', are we talking about a specific time period, how do we measure 'working-class' and 'middle-class' backgrounds and so on, but the statement is expressed in terms of a hypothesis.

An aim, on the other hand, is a statement of an intention to investigate or explore something. For example, an aim would be: 'To analyse the exam results of children from schools in predominantly working-class neighbourhoods and compare them with the exam results of children from schools in predominantly middle-class neighbourhoods to see whether any differences in exam performance emerge.'

Coursework exercise

Below are some aspects of sociology topics which you may have studied. For each one with which you are familiar, write down two possible hypotheses and two possible aims which could arise and which could provide the basis of an AS coursework task. Remember that the topic areas are expressed in quite broad terms, while your hypotheses and aims should have a much narrower focus. The most useful way of doing this is to take a sheet of A4 paper in the landscape format (turned so the longest sides are at the top and bottom), and rule it into three columns. In the first column, copy out the topic area as given below, and head the other two columns 'Possible hypotheses' and 'Possible aims', then fill in the blanks. One has been completed on page 100 as an example.

Topic areas

1 **State policies and the family**
2 **The diversity of contemporary family structure**
3 **Inequalities in access to healthcare**
4 **The public perception of mental illness**
5 **Media representations**

6 **The mass media and moral panics**

7 **Educational achievement and ethnicity**

8 **Pupils' perceptions of schooling**

9 **The nature and extent of poverty in contemporary Britain**

10 **The nature and role of voluntary welfare provision**

11 **The nature and extent of work satisfaction**

12 **The leisure patterns of teenagers**

Topic area	Possible hypotheses	Possible aims
State policies and the family	1 State policies on the family over the past ten years have been designed to promote the conventional nuclear family.	1 To investigate the nature of state policies on the family over the last ten years.
	2 State policies on the family do little to help women with dependent children to return to work.	2 To investigate the views of mothers with children under five on returning to paid employment.

Having decided on a suitable hypothesis or aim, you are also required in this first section to state your reasons for choosing both the general research issue and the specific hypothesis or aim. It is important that the reasons offered are clear, concise and sociological. Simply saying 'I am interested in this topic' is not sufficient, although this is likely to be one of the underlying reasons for your choice. You should try to identify what it is about the topic that arouses your interest. It may be, for example, that the sociological evidence you have looked at contradicts 'common sense' views on the topic, or it may reflect something from your own personal experience which you think is worthy of further study, or you may consider it to be an important social issue. Whatever reasons you give, these should be carefully thought out.

Research in Practice

Aretha had chosen to focus on the representations of people from ethnic minority groups in stories in national newspapers and on the television news. Below is the first draft of her section one, 'Hypothesis/Aims'.

Title: Media representations of people from ethnic minorities

My aim is to investigate how news stories in both national newspapers and on television news show people from ethnic minority groups. Media representations can be very powerful, and can influence how people in the wider society view particular groups. Media representations can be both positive and negative, but the sociological literature suggests that where ethnic minority groups are concerned, such representations are more likely to be negative than positive, reflecting the underlying racism of many people and groups in society.

I have chosen to investigate this topic because my study of this aspect of the sociology of the mass media has made me aware, as someone from an Afro-Caribbean background, that there are relatively few positive images of people from ethnic minority groups, particularly black and Asian groups, portrayed in the mainstream media.

(135 words)

Coursework exercise

1   Refer to the mark scheme for Section 1 of the AS coursework task and decide into which mark band this should be placed if Aretha were to leave it unaltered. (Note: in practice, the marker never marks one section without having read the whole piece through, as one of the most important aspects is the ability to progress the chosen hypothesis or aim through the whole proposal. Nevertheless, for the purpose of this exercise you should attempt to place the piece provisionally into one of the three mark bands.)

2   Note that Aretha has exceeded the word limit. Edit the draft to see whether you can reduce it to 100 words without losing any important points.

3   Suggest:
   a   two suitable pieces which Aretha might use as context for her study
   b   two concepts which would enable the research to be progressed
   c   a suitable method for conducting the proposed investigation, with reasons for your choice
   d   at least three potential problems.

   For b, state how each of the concepts you identify would inform the research study.

Research in Practice

Leo said that he had decided to take a topic from the area of 'education'. Here is his first draft of Section 1.

Title: 'I can't, Miss – it might mess up my hair'

I have decided to test the hypothesis that teenage boys at school are more into sport than girls, as girls worry about getting sweaty and mucky and messing up their hair and make-up. I have chosen this because I play a lot of sport, and so do my mates, but the PE teacher always has a load of trouble getting girls out onto the sports field, as they are always saying they've forgotten their kit, or it's PMT or something, while really, if you listen to them talking about it, they just don't want to run about and get mucky. Also, girls don't really know much about female sportswomen, so they don't look up to people like boys do with David Beckham or other famous footballers.

(126 words)

To give you a clue, Aretha's first draft showed promise. Below is a first draft from another student, Leo, which is less successful.

Coursework exercise

You will already have noticed that at first glance this isn't a sociological piece. Firstly, the title doesn't signal a clear sociological focus, and the hypothesis, which is in any event too long and cumbersome, doesn't appear to fit into the specification. The reasons given for the choice are anecdotal rather than sociological, while the last sentence doesn't follow logically from what has gone before.

However, with more thought (and probably more reading of sociological texts!) Leo could explore his chosen area. Below are some suggestions as to how this might be done. Read them carefully, then try to produce a second draft, within the 100 word limit, which Leo could show to his teacher and which should receive a more favourable response.

1   **Leave the title for the moment and come back to this when you have completed your draft, as the modified text might help you to identify a more suitable (and sociological) title.**

2   **Leo had said that the topic came from 'education'. If so, exactly where might this be? On the other hand, the topic might fit better with one of the core themes. Look at these and decide which one might be suitable.**

3   **Leo's proposed investigation of the sporting activities of teenage boys and girls at school is currently stated as a hypothesis. Rewrite this, taking care not to make it as rambling as the original. You might wish to re-read Leo's final sentence, as this might give you some ideas for a slightly different hypothesis. Having done that, now write an aim based on the same area. Look carefully at what you have written and decide whether you prefer the hypothesis or the aim, and say why.**

4   **Now think of some sociological reasons why this might be an important topic to explore, linking it to whichever area of the specification you have chosen. Are there any links to particular theories or perspectives which might be useful here?**

5   **Of course, no student should ever write the first section without having an overall plan of the whole coursework task. You should now, therefore, make brief notes on what you think Leo should do for the remaining sections. This means that you should identify:**
    a   two suitable pieces of context material (bearing in mind your chosen area of the specification)

A
B
C
D
E
F
G
H
I
J
K
L
M
N
O
P
Q
R
S
T
U
V
W
X
Y
Z

    b   two concepts which would inform the study

    c   a suitable method for carrying out the investigation, with reasons

    d   at least three potential problems which might occur if the investigation were carried out.

6   Now look at what you have written for a, b, c and d, and explain briefly how each one links clearly to the rewritten hypothesis or aim you produced for task 3.

7   Lastly, in the light of all that you have just written, come up with a suitable title which shows clearly the sociological focus of the proposed investigation.

15.7 Section 2: Context and concepts

Choosing appropriate pieces of material to use as your context is extremely important, and you should think carefully about this. The role of the context material is to place your proposed research within a sociological context. This means that the chosen contexts should contribute something to the debate in which your proposed research is located. For example, if your proposed research were something to do with gender differences in educational achievement, your context material could include two of the following: statistical data on examination results by gender; a research study into the area of differential educational achievement by gender; a newspaper report giving details of the current situation and suggesting some possible explanations, and so on. Note that one of the suggested pieces of context was from a newspaper rather than an obvious 'sociological' source. For the purposes of this task, official statistics would count as a sociological source, although you will be familiar with the problems of interpreting statistics. This does not mean, however, that they should not be used; in fact, many sociologists draw on official (and other) statistics as useful sources of data.

It is quite acceptable to use a non-sociological source for your context material, although it would perhaps be unwise if both your contexts were non-sociological. What you must do when explaining the significance of your context however, if you have chosen newspaper, magazine or television material, is to draw out its sociological significance with regard to your proposal. In other words, you must subject your non-sociological source material to a sociological analysis.

It is also important to remember that you do not submit your context material with your research proposal, so the marker does not get to see it. While many of the chosen pieces will be familiar to the examiner, some, particularly when chosen from a non-sociological source, will not, so you must be very clear and explicit about what the material is, and why it forms a suitable context for your proposed research.

The following checklist is a way of helping you to decide whether you have identified suitable pieces of context material and used them in an appropriate way.

✓ Checklist 5

Have I chosen suitable contexts?

	Completed	
	Yes	No
1 Is at least one of them from a 'sociological' source?	☐	☐
2 Have I given clear details of each, i.e. title, author, date, source?	☐	☐
3 Have I drawn out the important points about each with regard to how the material is linked to, and helps to inform, my proposed hypothesis/aim?	☐	☐
4 If I have used a non-sociological source, have I commented on it in a sociological manner, e.g. using appropriate sociological concepts?	☐	☐

Research in Practice

Nass had a research proposal on state policies and the family, based on a hypothesis that 'Recent Government policies on the family promote a particular type of family structure'. He came across an article in the *The Observer* newspaper (5 November 2000) part of which is reprinted below. He decided that this would form one of his two pieces of context material.

Official: marriage is the best
Newlyweds to be given state guidance

A Government-sponsored guide to the perfect marriage will be given to every couple planning a wedding, *The Observer* can reveal.

The controversial new book, which will include advice on what to wear and information that marriage can make you healthier, will be part of the Government's drive to promote marriage over other forms of family life.

But the plans for the book, which will be launched in the new year, were last night condemned by single-parent organisations and Labour MPs. 'Promoting marriage in this way is a cultural throwback,' said Katharine Stinson of the lone-parents group, Gingerbread. 'It feeds into the stereotype that there is a hierarchy of relationships. That is not the case.'

The book, called Married Life, is being put together by two government-funded organisations and the Archbishops' Council of the Church of England. The scheme is expected to cost up to £1 million a year. It was unclear last night how much taxpayers' money is going into the scheme.

The book will re-ignite the fierce debate on the Government's role in the nation's private life. The Government has been criticised in the past for taking on too many elements of the 'nanny state' with advice on how to bring up children and family life.

'Call me old-fashioned, but I believe that government should stick to the issues they really have an effect on, such as the quality of public housing or unemployment,' said Diane Abbott, the Labour backbencher.

'All the evidence shows the Government can't really affect long-term social trends and the long-term trend is to delay or turn away altogether from marriage.'

Coursework exercise

1 Taking the extract from *The Observer* newspaper article, write 75–100 words about it which would be suitable for the context and concepts section. Remember to acknowledge the origin of the material, to make your comments sociological, and keep in mind that the examiner will not be able to refer to the article.

2 Identify a suitable concept suggested by the material in the article, and write a brief definition, also saying why you think that this concept would be useful for Nass's proposed research.

3 Suggest a second piece of context material, this time from a 'sociological' source such as a textbook or research study.

4 Suggest a second concept which would inform the research proposal, again writing a brief definition and saying how the concept would be useful in collecting and/or analysing the data.

Once you have chosen suitable pieces of context material, it is important to focus carefully on your two concepts. Sometimes one or both of these will arise from your context material, though this will not necessarily be the case. One of the main points to bear in mind is how you would operationalise the concept if you were to carry out the research. If you choose an inappropriate concept when you are actually carrying out research, as in a piece of A2 coursework, you will quickly become aware of this. However, when what you are doing is making a research proposal without (at least at this stage) actually doing any research, it is harder to spot if either of your concepts is unsuitable in some way.

You have to spend some time thinking about this. One way is to use checklist 6 on page 109 for each of your chosen concepts.

Students often make two kinds of problems for themselves when choosing concepts. One is that they choose a concept such as 'gender' because it seems of obvious relevance. Sometimes, however, what is obvious may not be best. Remember that your research focus should be narrow, and sometimes it will be the case that another concept would be better than gender, such as 'ethnicity' or 'age'. If gender is not the most significant variable, including it often makes the research proposal more cumbersome, as the student thinks that because 'gender' is a chosen concept, any questionnaires or interviews must include men and women, to show any differences. It may be perfectly appropriate (and easier) to study only women (or only men) if gender is left out of the proposal.

Another way in which a problem can arise is when insufficient thought has been given to how a concept can be operationalised. Variables which are difficult to define or measure precisely come into this category. This includes things such as 'work satisfaction', 'good health care', 'racist attitudes', 'educational achievement' and so on. It does not mean that you should not use such variables – often they are eminently suitable for your proposed research. It does mean, however, that you should think carefully (and explain) how you would define and measure your chosen concept. It also means that in some cases the difficulty of operationalising the concept will appear as one of your 'potential problems', though you should have shown in the main research method and reasons section how you would attempt to do this.

✓ Checklist 6

Have I chosen suitable concepts?

	Completed	
	Yes	No

1 Am I clear that this concept is clearly linked to both the proposed area of research, and to my specific hypothesis/aim? ☐ ☐

2 Can I write a concise definition which is able to bring out the link to my proposed research? ☐ ☐

3 Can the concept be tracked through the hypothesis/aim, context and method? ☐ ☐

4 Would there be problems in operationalising the concept? ☐ ☐

5 Is there an aspect of the concept which might appear in the 'potential problems' section? (This does not have to be the case.) ☐ ☐

A B C D E F G H I J K L M N O P Q R S T U V W X Y Z

Research in Practice

Eloise was interested in the sociological literature (much of it from feminist sociologists writing in the 1980s) which explored sexism in schools and how it worked in a number of ways to the disadvantage of girls. Although she knew that things might have changed in many schools, and that girls were now generally out-performing boys in exams, she wondered whether many parents would still prefer to send their daughters to single-sex schools if they had the choice. She lived in an area in which there were both single-sex and co-educational schools, and decided on a research proposal which aimed to see whether parents of 10-year-old daughters had a preference for a particular type of secondary school and, very importantly, why.

Below is the first draft of her context and concepts section. Read it through, and then do the Coursework exercises which follow.

My first piece of context material is 'Gender and schooling: a study of sexual divisions in the classroom', by Michelle Stanworth (1983). I have chosen this as it contains interesting empirical material about teachers' attitudes and behaviour towards females in mixed-sex humanities classes. The conclusion from this would be that, under these circumstances, girls would benefit from being taught in single-sex institutions, or at least single-sex lessons. Although the situation may have changed, this work is still relevant as it is possible that some parents still believe that their daughters would do better academically at a girls-only school.

My second context document is a collection of educational league tables for secondary schools in 2002. I would use the tables to identify the top ten schools in the independent and state sector, for secondary schools in this area. I would see what proportion of the top ten in each category were single-sex and mixed. I know which schools are single-sex and which are mixed in this area, and I want to use the tables to see whether parents' perceptions of which would be 'good schools' for their daughters are actually borne out by the position of these schools in the league tables.

Continued

My first concept is gender. This means things associated with being either male or female. I would use this concept to explore in my interviews whether parents saw 'gender' as an issue when deciding on the best secondary school to send their daughters to.

My second concept is stereotype. This means holding certain beliefs about a group or category and applying these beliefs to anyone in that group or category. Stereotypes are can be positive or negative. I would use this concept to explore in my interviews whether the parents in the sample held particular stereotypes about both single-sex and mixed-sex schools, and whether these stereotypes were negative or positive.

(Number of words: 313)

Coursework exercise

1   Write brief comments about Eloise's choice of context material, saying whether you think each one provides a clear context for her aim, and explaining why or why not.

2   For each piece of context material proposed by Eloise, state whether you think that she has shown sufficient knowledge and understanding, and explain why or why not.

3   Suggest at least one (two if you can) other piece of suitable context material that Eloise might have used.

4   Write brief comments about Eloise's choice of concepts, saying whether you think each is appropriate, and why or why not.

5   For each concept, say whether you think Eloise has written an appropriate definition in the context of her research proposal.

6   Suggest two other concepts that Eloise might have used, defining each of them and saying how they could be used to inform the research proposal.

7   Note that Eloise has not reached the maximum word length (400) for
     this section. Note also that this doesn't matter – 400 words is a
     maximum, not a minimum. However, read through the draft again to
     see whether there is anything else which Eloise might have put in,
     making sure that you do not exceed 400 words overall.

8   Using the mark scheme, decide on the band into which you think
     Eloise's work should be placed, giving your reasons.

15.8 Section 3: Main research method and reasons

In this section of your coursework task, you must decide on the method that
you would choose if your research proposal were actually going to be carried
out. Note the word used is 'method' in the singular. This is because you are
required to select only one method. You may consider that the research would
be more valid if more than method were used, but for the purposes of the
coursework task you have to decide on just one method. If appropriate, in the
potential problems section, you could explain the shortcomings of using just
one method, but you will need to explain carefully why you think this is the
case. Remember the examiner is not expecting you to do this – one method
is all that is required and you need not mention others.

In your course, you will have studied all the methods used by sociologists to
gather data and learned about the strengths and weaknesses of each. In this
section, you will focus on the strengths of your chosen method, as you will be
explaining why you think it is the most suitable approach. An important point
is that it will not be sufficient simply to write out the general strengths of the
particular method chosen. Your task is to explain why you think it is the best
method to research your particular hypothesis or aim. In other words, the
strengths of the method must be applied to your particular research proposal.
Again, if you decide that there are some potential problems arising from the
use of this method, things of which a researcher should be aware, then these
should be stated in the potential problems section. The examiner will be
looking to see whether you have not just said why, for example, structured
interviews are a useful method, but why structured interviews are particularly
suitable for gathering the data needed for your chosen investigation. In
discussing your choice of method, you will therefore need to display
knowledge and understanding of both the method itself, and of its application
to a particular piece of research.

✓ Checklist 7

Have I chosen the most suitable method?

		Completed	
		Yes	No
1	Have I considered carefully all the sociological methods I have studied in my course?	☐	☐
2	Have I thought about the strengths and weaknesses of each?	☐	☐
3	Have I decided which method would be most suitable to my proposed research?	☐	☐
4	Have I been able to identify several reasons why this method would be most suitable with regard to my chosen hypothesis/aim?	☐	☐
5	Have I considered all the potential problems of using this method to research my chosen hypothesis/aim?	☐	☐
6	Having done that, am I still convinced that I have chosen the most suitable method for my proposed hypothesis/aim?	☐	☐

A B C D E F G H I J K L M N O P Q R S T U V W X Y Z

In addition to describing the method and reasons for your choice, this section requires you to give appropriate details on how the method would be implemented if the proposed research were carried out. It is in this discussion that the application of the method to your particular research project is drawn out. The details you need to provide will depend on both your chosen method and the particular research focus. Depending on these, you need to provide details of aspects such as the sampling frame, the type of sample to be drawn, the size of the sample, the type of question on the questionnaire or interview schedule (e.g. mainly closed or open-ended), the main areas on which questions would be focused, the type of observation (overt or covert), how you would gain access to the group to be studied, over how long a period your data would be gathered, which publications would form the basis of your secondary data, how the data would be analysed, and so on. You will, of course, select only those details which are relevant to your chosen method and research focus.

Research in Practice

Kemal had chosen the topic area of the mass media for his research proposal. The students in his sociology classs had been discussing a *Sociology Review* article about girls' magazines. Kemal found the article very interesting and had enjoyed the class discussion about it. He had therefore chosen the following aim for his research proposal: 'To find out what genres of magazines are read by 16–18-year-old males.' Below is Kemal's first draft of section three, main research method and reasons. Read it carefully and then do the coursework exercises which follow.

I have decided that the most appropriate method to investigate my stated aim would be a questionnaire. This is because it would generate a large amount of quantitative data on the typical reading habits of a sample of 16–18-year-old males. Analysis of these data would hopefully generate a further aim or hypothesis which could form the basis of a later piece of research, of a more qualitative nature.

I am aware that questionnaires, especially if they contain mainly closed questions, as mine would, are open to the criticism that the quantitative information they provide is of limited use, as it tells us 'what' but

Continued

does not tell us 'why'. However, in this case, it is the 'what' that I am interested in, namely what kind of magazines are typically read by young men. Both quantitative and qualitative research methods have their place in sociology and neither should be dismissed. The starting point has to be what the sociologist is trying to find out.

Part of my sample would be drawn from male students at my college. This would be relatively easy to do, but information obtained from this group might not be reliable, as college students might have reading tastes different from other young men. The second sample would therefore be obtained by standing in a large newsagents from a national chain and asking young men in the shop, who were of the right age group, if they would answer the questions on the questionnaire. I would need to include a question on the questionnaire about what the respondents did, as some of them would probably be college students. Hopefully though, I would obtain a cross section. As the questionnaires would be relatively quick to answer and also to analyse, I would do 40 from the college sample and 40 from the newsagent sample.

To draw up the questionnaire, I would first look in several newsagents to identify the magazines which seemed to be aimed mainly at males or equally at both sexes, and classify them into different genres, such as sport, music, hobbies and male interest. Under these headings I would list the different magazines, and also include a space where respondents could mention the titles of any not on the list. I would also ask how frequently the respondent read the magazine. I would need to ask about reading rather than buying, as they might read something which was at home because it was bought by their father or brother rather than themselves. I would also include an open-ended question about what it was about the magazines they read that they particularly liked, and whether they read all the content or only certain sections, and if so, which ones.

453 words

Coursework exercise

1 What is meant by 'quantitative data'?

2 Explain what Kemal means when he says that his questionnaire would contain 'mainly closed questions'.

3 Give an example of a qualitative research method.

4 Explain why sociologists might wish to use 'a sample' in their research.

5 Explain what Kemal means when he says that information obtained from the college students 'might not be reliable'.

6 Suggest what Kemal might use as a sampling frame for his sample of college students.

7 Describe a suitable sampling method for choosing the college sample, saying why you think it is suitable.

8 Identify two problems which Kemal might encounter when choosing his sample of young men in the newsagents.

9 What kind of sample would Kemal be likely to use for his newsagent group?

10 Identify two problems with Kemal's description of the open-ended question at the end of his questionnaire.

11 Re-write Kemal's draft so that it falls within the 400 word limit. Try not simply to cut out parts, but see whether there are parts which could be summarised.

12 Look at the mark scheme and decide into which band Kemal's work should go, giving reasons for your decision.

One of the main tasks in this section is to provide convincing reasons why the chosen method and your explanations are clearly appropriate to your particular hypothesis or aim. This is another example of how important it is to choose wisely when deciding on your hypothesis or aim, and how you have to make sure that this is carried through all the sections of the coursework task. Use checklist 7 on page 113 to help you decide whether you have chosen the most suitable method.

15.9 Section 4: Potential problems

In this section, you are required to identify aspects of the proposed research study which might be problematic. In other words, if the research were carried out in the way described in the proposal, what kinds of issues would the sociologist need to bear in mind and what pitfalls would she need to avoid?

You will have learned by now that all sociological research methods (indeed, all research methods, whether in sociology or any other discipline) are potentially problematic, or have certain possible disadvantages of which the researcher needs be aware. However, in this section it is not sufficient simply to come up with a learned list of 'the disadvantages of method X'. You will have to show how the potential problems you identify apply *in the context of researching your chosen hypothesis and aim*. In other words, your discussion must be specific to your particular research proposal, and not general to the method you have chosen.

Areas which are potentially problematic include aspects of:

- **ethics**
- **time**
- **cost**
- **sampling**
- **access (to a particular group, a suitable location, or particular documents)**
- **reliability**
- **validity.**

Research in Practice

Patti was interested in the issue of 'labelling' in schools.
She had enjoyed studying this part of the education topic,
and had become aware of a situation in her own school
which she thought would provide the basis of an
interesting research proposal. Her school had an 'open
sixth form', which meant that students were admitted to
the sixth form without necessarily having a certain
number of GCSEs at certain grades. Lack of employment
opportunities in her town meant that quite a large
number of students who had not done particularly well at
GCSE (for a variety of reasons) stayed on into the sixth
form to try to improve their qualifications and hopefully
their job prospects. These students followed a special
programme for part of their curriculum, mainly designed
to improve their basic numeracy and literacy skills, with
some of them also doing a subject at GNVQ Intermediate
level. The rest of their programme involved them in the
same classes as students doing AS/A levels, such as sport,
general studies, work experience in the community and
health education.

Patti had noticed, however, that these students were not
socially integrated into the sixth form, but tended to
remain apart in separate small groups, even in the joint
activities, and she had overheard them referred to by
some of the other students in quite negative ways, such
as 'the thickies'.

She had decided to investigate why the students following
'academic' subjects held such negative stereotypes of the
group, and also to find out from the students in the group
how they saw themselves, what they thought of the other
sixth-form students and why they seldom mixed with
them. Her aim was, 'To explore some of the causes and
consequences of labelling among sixth-form students.' Her
chosen method was to conduct semi-structured interviews
with open-ended questions. A sample of 'academic' sixth-
form students would be interviewed singly, while, in order
to give them greater confidence, the other students would
be interviewed in pairs or groups of three. Patti's concepts
were 'labelling' and 'self-image'.

Coursework exercise

1 Identify two **ethical** problems which Patti might include in section four, making sure to offer 'appropriate, accurate and succinct' reasons for your choice.

2 State why **reliability** might be identified as a potential problem, again making sure to give reasons, as above.

3 Identify two **practical** problems which might arise from the process of interviewing the two groups of students.

4 Identify two problems which might arise regarding the **analysis** and **interpretation** of the data collected.

5 Imagining that you are Patti, write section four, being sure to stick to the 300 word limit. You may be able to identify potential problems in addition to those mentioned above.

You will need to think very carefully about your proposed research to identify all the potential problems. Note that you do not have to state how you might resolve the problems – the issue is whether and how well you are able to relate general problems of methodology to a particular research issue. Your ability to do this will display the degree of sociological insight you have developed, and is important to your development of the skill of evaluation. It will help you to look more critically at any research study you come across in your study of sociology.

Of course, you do not simply have to *identify* the potential problems, but also to explain why they might be problems. In the words of the mark scheme, you have to offer 'appropriate, accurate and succinct reasons'; the word limit does not allow you to waffle!

Remember the important point that, although the coursework task is presented in four separate sections, it should be a unified whole, and everything in it should relate back to your hypothesis or aim. This is as true of this section as it is of all the others, so when considering the potential problems, make your starting point your own hypothesis/aim rather than focusing only on the method you have chosen.

The OCR AS research report

The OCR AS research report has several distinct features. These include:

- **a class-based task with no requirement to carry out any primary research**
- **a choice between a sociological study, other pieces of coursework or a media item as the basis of the critique**
- **a required structure into sections**
- **a maximum recommended word length**
- **an opportunity to use the AS research report as a basis for the A2 personal study.**

16.1 Choice of study

The aim of the research report is to introduce you to the problems and opportunities of sociological research, so that if you choose, you will be able to implement the lessons that you have learned in your A2 personal study (see 16.4). You are not required to engage in the actual research process yourself, although if your teacher has used the opportunity of the substantive topics of modules 1 and 2 to allow you to carry out some practice research, you should bring that experience to bear on the research report. For example, if you have studied 'the family' in Module 2, you may have been asked to carry out a small-scale questionnaire with members of your family, or conduct an oral history with one of your grandparents.

You have to write your research report on one of the following.

1. **A piece of completed sociological research, which can be:**
   - **a full-length book (but this is not expected or required)**
   - **an article from a sociological journal, such as the *British Journal of Sociology of Education***
   - **an article from a sociology magazine such as *Sociology Review***

   • summaries of research found in sociology textbooks.

2 A piece of completed coursework, which can be:

   • a project completed by a previous sociology coursework student, or by students from another school or college

   • a project which you and your colleagues have completed as part of your sociology course.

3 A piece of completed research that has sociological interest, which can be:

   • a newspaper article

   • a media programme, such as a documentary.

In all cases, you should ensure that the piece chosen has an identifiable methodology, a statement of aims and objectives, and a report of the findings, so that a proper account and evaluation may be given (see 16.2).

16.2 Structure of the research report

All research reports have to be organised in the following format:

1 The source of the research
   This includes, title, author, publication date and publisher, if appropriate. There are conventions for presenting these and sociologists mainly use the Harvard system. This would present this book as:

   Garrod, J., Clynch, A. and Lawson T., 2003, *A–Z Sociology Coursework Handbook* London Hodder & Stoughton

2 The research objective
   You must write what the purpose of the research was. This must be done in your own words, as you need to avoid the charge of plagiarism.

3 An outline of the methodology
   You need to identify the method or methods chosen by the writer, including such aspects, where appropriate, as access, sample size, specific research instruments used, degree of participation and any special features.

4 Reasons for the selection of the methodology
   You should suggest why you think the particular strategy was adopted, using any clues in the piece of research itself. As a general guide, you should cover:

- **theoretical considerations**
- **practical constraints**
- **ethical issues**

that might have informed the choices made.

5 **An outline and evaluation of the findings of the research**
You should summarise in your own words the main findings of the research and offer a limited set of the data included. As you are advised on word length for each section, you should not be too ambitious in providing the data themselves. Rather, it is necessary in this section to assess the importance of the findings in order to meet AO2 skills (see 16.3). In doing so, you might want to refer to:

- **the limitations of the methodology used**
- **how other methods might have strengthened the findings.**

16.3 Word lengths and assessment objectives

OCR provide suggested word lengths for each of the main sections of the research report, within an overall target of 1000 words. The suggested lengths are:

- **Research objective: 10–30 words**
- **Outline of research methodology: 200–270 words**
- **Reasons for selection of methodology: 250–300 words**
- **Outline and evaluation of findings: 350–400 words**

To keep within these limits, you must ensure that you only include relevant comments, and resist the desire to 'write all you know' about methods. A focused report is more valuable than a long rambling one.

The assessment objectives and marks for the research report are:

AO1 (Knowledge, understanding, presentation)		48 marks
AO2 (Interpretation, analysis, evaluation)		42 marks
	Total	90 marks

Note that AO1 has slightly more marks available than AO2. This is because it is AS work; these proportions are reversed in A2 work.

16.4 Using the research report to support A2 personal study

Though it is not a requirement of the research report, you can choose to use it as a first step towards the personal study in A2. It is always a good idea to choose an area from sociology that you are interested in for your coursework, as this will help you to enjoy the process and retain motivation. However, if you are fairly certain that you want to follow through this interest into your personal study, then choose to do a research report on a major piece of work in this area. You can also use the research report to identify some of the issues and problems associated with different methodologies, so that you can avoid some of the basic mistakes when you come to do your own primary research for the A2 personal study. However, you are not committed to doing anything in A2 by your choices in AS. If you come across an area you find more interesting as the course develops, you can switch strategies and let your research report stand alone.

16.5 How to make best use of your teacher

Your teacher has three important roles with respect to your AS research report.

1 **You must seek the approval of your teacher for your chosen piece of completed research. Indeed, some teachers may offer you a limited choice from which to choose. If you decide that you want to do something else, you will have to gain the permission and approval of your teacher. This rule is to ensure that your choice fulfils the criteria and contains all the elements that it needs to.**

2 **Your teacher will be a good source of guidance and monitoring during the AS coursework and in particular will help you with the planning for and timing of carrying out the report.**

3 **Your teacher also marks the research report, which is then externally moderated by OCR, so it is best that she or he knows what you have been attempting to do during its compilation.**

✓Checklist

The following checklists will help you to ensure that you have done everything that you need to do for your AS or A2 coursework. As you complete a task, put a tick in the box. You may not necessarily complete the tasks in the order in which they appear.

AQA AS COURSEWORK TASK

1   Am I quite clear about what the Coursework Task involves? ☐

2   Do I know the deadline by which my research proposal has to be handed in for marking? ☐

   (This date is ………………………..)

3   Have I got a copy of the mark scheme so I know how my work will be assessed? ☐

4   Am I clear about the maximum number of words for each section? ☐

5   Have I identified a sociological focus for my research which falls within the specification? ☐

6   Have I developed an appropriate hypothesis or aim? ☐

7   Have I identified two suitable pieces of context, at least one of which is from a 'sociological' source? ☐

8   Have I chosen two suitable concepts which would help to inform the research? ☐

9   Would I be able to operationalise these concepts if I were to carry out the research? ☐

10 Have I chosen a suitable method? ☐

11 Am I able to explain why I consider that the method I havechosen is the most suitable to investigate my hypothesis/aim? ☐

12 Have I identified potential problems that might arise if this research were to be carried out? ☐

13 Have I produced a first draft and discussed this with my teacher?

14 Have I checked the number of words in each section? ☐

15 Have I completed and signed my Candidate Record Form? ☐

Continued

OCR AS RESEARCH REPORT

1 Am I quite clear about what the research report requires me to do? ☐

2 Do I know the deadline by which the research report has to be handed in for marking? ☐

(This date is ....)

3 Have I got a copy of the Assessment Matrix so I know how my work will be assessed? ☐

4 Am I clear about the recommended word limits for the different sections? ☐

5 Does my chosen research have sufficient information to enable me to comment on the main research objectives? ☐

6 Does my chosen research have sufficient information to enable me to comment on the research methodology? ☐

7 Does my chosen research have sufficient information to enable me to comment on the reasons for deciding on the methodology? ☐

8 Does my chosen research have sufficient information to enable me to comment on the findings of the research? ☐

9 Have I produced a draft research report and discussed this with my teacher? ☐

AQA A2 COURSEWORK

1 Am I quite clear about what the A2 coursework involves? ☐

2 Do I know the deadline by which my work has to be handed in for marking? ☐

(This date is ....)

3 Have I got a copy of the appropriate mark scheme (primary or secondary data) so I know how my work will be assessed? ☐

4 Am I clear about the recommended maximum word length of 3500 words? ☐

✓ **Continued**

5   Have I identified a sociological focus for my research which falls within the specification? ☐

6   Have I started my research diary? ☐

7   Have I chosen a suitable working title? ☐

8   Have I developed an appropriate hypothesis or aim? ☐

9   Have I written the Rationale section? ☐

10   Have I written the Context section? ☐

11   Have I written the Methodology section? ☐

12   Have I written the Evidence section? ☐

13   Have I written the Evaluation section? ☐

14   Have I listed all the sources I have used in the Bibliography section? ☐

15   Have I numbered all the pages? ☐

16   Have I included an index? ☐

17   Have I included a page from my research diary? ☐

18   Have I put my name, candidate number and centre number on the front cover? ☐

19   Have I completed and signed my Candidate Record Form? ☐

OCR A2 PERSONAL STUDY

1   Am I quite clear about what writing the Personal Study involves? ☐

2   Have I discussed my ideas for the personal study with my teacher? ☐

3   Do I know the deadline by which the outline of my personal tudy must be submitted for approval? ☐

(This date is ……………………………..)

4   Have I got a copy of the Assessment Matrix so I know how my work will be assessed? ☐

5   Am I clear about the recommended guidelines for the word lengths of the different sections? ☐

Continued

6. Do I know the deadline by which my work must be handed in for marking?

   (This date is ....)

7. Have I chosen an appropriate title?

8. Have I started my research diary?

9. Have I written the Rationale section?

10. Have I written the Research section and organised it under suitable sub-headings?

11. Have I written the Evaluation section?

12. Have I included a list of all the sources I have used in a Bibliography?

13. Have I included one copy of the required documents in the Appendix?

14. Have I included my research diary?

15. Have I handed in all other materials (the Annexe) to be kept in a safe place in case they are needed?

A B C D E F G H I J K L M N O P Q R S T U V W X Y Z

Using information and communications technology for your coursework

The usefulness of information and communications technology (ICT) for your coursework has increased as the applications for which it can be used have expanded. Information and communications technology (more precisely technologies) refers to the ability of computer hardware and software to record, handle, present and transfer information or data. You are already likely to have come across information technology (IT) in school, perhaps using computers in science lessons, or even on special IT courses. In IT, the focus is on the skills and understanding needed to know when to use information and communications technology effectively. This might include keyboard skills (using the keyboard and mouse to achieve desired effects) or problem-solving skills (knowing when to use and when not to use a particular application to meet a specific need you have). Information and communications technology refers to the facilities (applications and software) which can be used to support your learning and the ways in which you can demonstrate your learning to others.

17.1 Definitions

Applications are the general (or generic) uses to which specific software may be put, for example, wordprocessing, information handling, electronic communications. Each application will cover many different pieces of software which can all carry out much the same functions. Most people end up with a favourite piece of software to carry out each application, usually because it is the one they are most used to.

Software are the specific programmes, usually produced and sold by a commercial firm (but sometimes given free) which can be used to carry out an application. For example, with wordprocessing, you may have come across Microsoft Word, which is the wordprocessing application produced by the giant software company Microsoft. There is other wordprocessing software available however, such as WordPerfect. While particular pieces of software may differ in specific ways, once you understand the basic principles of an application, it is usually relatively easy to use a different brand, without too much frustration.

17.2 What should you use and how should you use it?

The major ICT applications which might be useful to you are:

* **wordprocessing**
* **spreadsheets**
* **graphics packages**
* **access to the Internet and the World Wide Web**
* **electronic mail facilities**
* **databases or hypertext systems**
* **CD-ROMs**
* **videoconferencing.**

These are arranged in descending order of likely use, with the most frequently used at the top of the list.

Basically, you can use ICT for your coursework in four ways:

* **for gathering information or data**
* **for managing and tracking the collection of information and data**
* **for analysing the data**
* **for presenting your coursework and data.**

17.3 Gathering information using ICT

Once you have determined your area of study, you will want to collect as much information about it as possible, to help you with your context (AQA; AS and A2). Much of the information you acquire will be from sociological books, such as the major textbooks, accounts of original research or books which cover a particular topic in sociology. One of the problems with such texts is that they are inevitably out-of-date, because of the time it takes to write and publish such material. Recent developments in ICT allow you to look for and find contemporary material on a vast range of subjects, often with just a few clicks of the mouse.

CD-ROMs

The first source of material is ready-made and comes in the form of CD-ROMs. These are compact discs for the computer, which can contain huge amounts of information about particular topics. The advantage of CD-ROMs over textbooks is that they are not restricted to the written word, but may include sound, visual and graphical material as well, with which the user can often interact. They are easy to use and search through and they are also fairly reliable sources of information.

The disadvantage with CD-ROMs from a sociology coursework point of view is that there are hardly any, as yet, written specifically for sociologists. Another problem is that you are likely to be dependent on what your school or college has purchased, how old their version is and how easy it is to gain access to it. If you do have your own CD-ROMs (many computer firms give you free encyclopaedia CD-ROMs when you buy one of their computers) check through to see if there is any useful information on them for your coursework. Buying a CD-ROM is likely to prove costly if all you want it for is your sociology project.

However, these disadvantages should not put you off exploring the possibilities of CD-ROMs. General encyclopaedia CD-ROMs (such as *Encarta*) contain much up-to-date information of use to the sociologist. More recent versions of *Encarta* and other encyclopaedia CD-ROMs also have links to the Internet built into their information, so that you can move out into the World Wide Web through links which are guaranteed to be about the particular topic in which you are interested.

In exploring the possibilities of CD-ROMs you will need to know which ones are available in your school or college, where they are located and how you gain access. You will also need to have some basic IT skills to load and use CD-ROMs. However, as long as you can move a mouse to point and click your cursor, you should have little trouble. It may be that you are restricted to using CD-ROMs in particular locations or using only specific computers. Check out your library resource centre or IT centre to see what is available. You should also ask your sociology teacher if there are any CD-ROMs in the department and which one(s) she or he would recommend. A particularly useful CD-ROM is one produced by the government called *Social Trends*, which contains all the social statistics which have been gathered by various government agencies over a set period of time.

The Internet and the World Wide Web

The Internet is a complex network of computer networks, all linked up to each other through telephone lines, cables and via satellite. Situated on all these computers are the millions of pages of information which go together to make up the World Wide Web. Because there are agreed ways of putting information on the Web (they are called internet protocols and HTML or hyper text markup language is an example, if you are interested in that sort of thing), very different computers and pieces of software can 'talk' to each other. The importance of this is that you can link across the globe to any website that is sitting on a computer, at any time of the day or night. You can access the Internet through school, college or home if there is a connection to it.

At home, this might be through a computer modem, which is connected to your telephone line or to cable if it is available. At the other end of your connection is an Internet service provider (ISP) who provides you with a route into the World Wide Web. Be careful to establish with whoever pays for your connection what the rules of access are. For example, if you are connected through a home telephone line, then 'surfing' the Internet can block callers trying to reach your home number. Having two telephone lines, or cable capability, overcomes this problem, but remember that time spent on the Internet has to be paid for and therefore there may be restrictions on when you can use it and for how long.

Schools and colleges are increasingly connected to the Internet through a variety of means. The government has provided all schools and colleges with the finance to establish Internet links, as it sees the Internet as an important tool in education. However, some types of connection are more expensive than others. The general rule is that the greater the speed of the connection and the greater the number of machines networked to the connection, the more costly it is to pay for the connection. You may not be bothered about the cost (because you will not have to pay for it yourself), but you will be affected by the bandwidth of your institution's connection (the broader the bandwidth, the quicker information downloads to your machine) and the number of connected computers in your school (the more that are networked the less likely you are to have to wait for a computer to become available).

The first thing you have to do then is check out when and where you are able to use computers to access the Internet. Different schools and colleges will have different arrangements. Some will only allow supervised access in normal lessons. Others will allow access at any time for individuals, even extending

A B C D E F G H I J K L M N O P Q R S T U V W X Y Z

beyond the school day. Some will have a booking system, others will operate a 'first-come, first-served' system. Whichever works in your school or college, the implication is that you will have to plan to use the Internet in a systematic way to ensure that you gather information for your coursework at an appropriate time, and not at the last minute. Remember that you are unlikely to find all the information you want in only one session, no matter how long it is.

The second thing you must find out about is your school or college's 'acceptable use policy'. As there is very little control over what can be posted on the World Wide Web, there are sites which your parents, teachers, the government and you yourself might consider unsuitable. Most attention has been paid to pornographic sites, but there are also 'hate' sites and 'terrorist' sites which can offend or give access to information which is dangerous. These sites are a consequence of the freedom of speech associated with the World Wide Web, and given the nature of the Web it is unlikely that they can be controlled by anybody. However, although such sites may very occasionally be accidentally accessed, hits on unsuitable sites are mostly the result of choices made by the person using the Internet. So, nearly all pornographic sites have warning pages associated with them and a user would have to choose to ignore the warning to gain access.

All schools and colleges will likely have a stated policy (often called 'acceptable use policy' or AUP) which defines what is and what is not acceptable for students using their computers to access on the Internet. For example, some schools and colleges have decided to regulate the use of chat lines so that they are not permitted during school hours, or only allowed under certain conditions (for example when work is completed). While there are likely to be different policies for different age groups, access to unsuitable sites will be restricted and penalties imposed on offenders (these usually involving removing access privileges and informing parents of infringements). Some schools and colleges have invested in filtering software which only allows access to certain approved sites or prevents access to other sites either by web address or the presence of certain words in the web pages.

However, there are disadvantage in restricting access (especially through filtering software) which are particularly pertinent for sociologists engaged in coursework. Filtering software is a very crude device in dealing with unsuitable sites. It not only excludes sites which can be of no interest to the serious sociologist, but also sites which may be central to your coursework. The classic example is of software which prevents access to any site containing the word 'gay'; this has the effect of excluding most serious sites on the issue of AIDS.

Moreover, any restriction on access goes against the philosophy of free speech which is at the heart of the World Wide Web. Those who defend free speech on the Internet argue for a policy of responsible use rather than censorship. You must think carefully about your own use of the Internet and how responsible your choices are as you surf it, especially if you are researching areas which might bring you inadvertently into contact with unsuitable sites. For example, if you are interested in racism, you are likely to come across some hate sites in the course of your research. You must decide how essential your access to such sites is for your coursework and not just give in to curiosity without thinking of the possible penalties which you might attract. If in doubt, seek advice from your teacher or the person responsible for supervising the ICT facilities.

Once you have established the rules of access, what facilities are available to you through the school's connection? The main advantage of being connected is the ability to open up the millions of pages of information 'freely' available to the surfer. To be able to do this, you will need to use browser software. This will be provided for you by your school or college when you access the Internet. The two main browsers are Netscape Navigator and Microsoft's Internet Explorer. These allow you to explore the WWW in different ways.

'Surfing the net' suggests a rather haphazard approach to gaining information from the Web, hinting at an unplanned, inquisitive approach, following the links from one web page to another, as your fancy takes you. The power of the WWW is that links are made between, perhaps geographically distant, but topically related sites which can be followed through a simple clicking of the cursor on a button (see Figure 17.1).

Figure 17.1

Indeed one of the criticisms of the Internet is that the surfer can waste enormous amounts of time (and money) simply following links without gathering any useful information. However this 'information overload' situation can be combated by 'smart surfing', that is, using the features of the net to develop strategies which should lead you to the information you require. There are three main strategies which you can use to gain relevant information:

- **knowing an Internet site address**
- **using an appropriate gateway**
- **using a search engine.**

1 Knowing an address

Every website on the Internet has a distinct URL (universal resource locator) which always begins with <http://>. Note that the symbols <...> here are not part of the address, but a convention to show where the address begins and ends. The URL for the University of Leicester is <http://www.le.ac.uk/>. There are reasons why the address has this particular form, but you do not need to worry about them. The important thing is that if you type this URL into the appropriate place on your browser and press Return, you will gain access to the front page of the University of Leicester website. You will find lists of useful sociology websites with their addresses on pages 215–217. One type of web posting that might be very useful to you is the electronic journals which now appear on the WWW. Look for some sociology journals (for example, *Sociology Online*) and see if there are any articles which might help you with your coursework. Remember that these articles are written for an academic audience and that they may be pitched at a difficult level. But you can always ask for some assistance if you come across ideas or concepts which are new to you. You never know, they might be just the ones you are looking for.

2 Using an appropriate gateway

Some web pages consist of lists of links which a surfer with a particular interest might find useful. For sociology, one of the main gateways is called SOSIG–the Social Science Information Gateway. (some people pronounce this as sos-ig, others as sausage!) you will find SOSIG at <http://www.sosig.co.uk/>. This gateway covers all the social sciences and you will need to click through the categories of subjects and topics until you come up with the list of links that take you to sites which cover your particular coursework focus. Because you are likely to use SOSIG many times, there is a facility to identify it as a frequently visited site. This is called 'bookmarks' in Navigator and 'favorites' in Explorer. When you have added the SOSIG site to your bookmarks (the button appears at the top of your screen), you just go back to the bookmark to return there at any time.

SOSIG is an invaluable help to the serious sociologist, but remember that it cannot hope to cover all the relevant information that you might need for your coursework. For example, you might want some information that is not just sociological, but of more general interest, such as information about a television programme on the BBC. Other social science gateways will go beyond sociological sites to give you access to wider information. One such is the website of the Association for the Teaching of the Social Sciences at <http://www.atss.org.uk/sites.html> (see Figure 17.2).

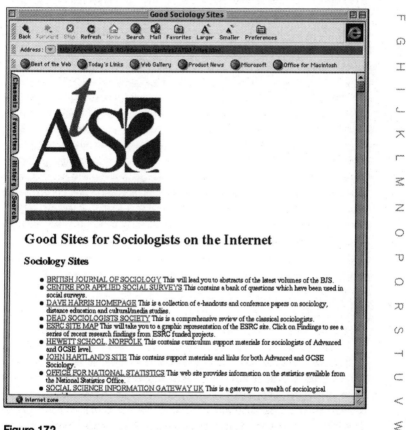

Figure 17.2

3 Using a search engine

There are various search engines available to you (different schools and colleges will have access to different ones) such as Google <http://www.google.co.uk> and Webcrawler <http://www. webcrawler.com/>. Though they all work in slightly different ways (some are more like gateways than search engines), the basic principles are the same. You put in a search term which you think covers the areas you are interested in, for example 'sociology family'. Press the search button and a list will appear which includes sites which contain those terms, often in a rank order, so that the most likely sites appear first.

However, it is important to realise that search engines are blunt instruments, mainly because they are searching millions of items of information all the time. Though they are getting smarter, it is more than likely that most of the links displayed will not be terribly useful for your coursework. Try some of them to see. If they are not useful you will need to refine your search term by finding more specific words or using synonyms (alternative words which mean the same as your original search term) or using Boolean logic. Boolean logic is just a way of making more conditions for the search. So, 'sociology family' would bring up links which included **either** sociology or the family. By typing in 'sociology AND family', you will **only** get the links which have **both** the words in. This more sophisticated approach operates to restrict the number of hits you will get. The + sign does something similar in some search engines when it is placed directly in front of a word. The Boolean operator OR expands a search to include both/all words indicated. For example, the search 'family OR husband OR wife' will hit any site with **any** of those terms in. You can use AND NOT (or a minus sign) to restrict searches further, so that 'family AND NOT husband' will only hit those sites where the word family appears without the word husband.

17.4 What do you do once you have found some useful information?

Remember that you will probably look at lots of web pages before you find some information which might help you with your coursework. You can try to cut down on your search time by focusing on the types of site which might turn up the right kind of information. Electronic sociology journals can usually be relied upon to have up-to-date research and ideas in particular sociology areas. Some journals are free to all surfers, while others will only give you abstracts and want a subscription for access to the full text. You are unlikely to be able to afford such subscriptions, even if you wanted to subscribe, but even the abstracts can give ideas and information. University sociology departments, both here and throughout the world (especially in the USA) are often sources of sociological information. Many sites of this type are more recruitment pages than providers of coursework information. Increasingly, schools and their sociology departments are posting useful information on the Web and you might find some of these relevant to your project. Organisations associated with your area of interest, such as charities or pressure groups, might also provide you with an interesting read. If your coursework is focused on a particular organisation, such as the Labour or Conservative party, then a visit to their website is a must.

Once you are at a useful site, you can just read the information that is available, but the more sensible option is to print it off and read it at your own convenience and without accruing cost to the school. You can print material from the Web using the usual print options on your screen. Material posted on the Web is to all intents and purposes (unless otherwise stated), copyright free, but the polite thing to do if you are going to use other people's material is to reference it correctly. The conventions of politeness used on the Internet are called netiquette and this has established various ways of referencing Web materials. You should include, where possible, the title of the pages, their author(s), their URL and the date it was last accessed by you. It is therefore important to remember to record in your coursework diary the URL of any Web page you might use in your coursework, as the address does not always appear on your print-out and websites constantly change.

This brings us to the most important piece of advice about using information from the Web. It is not enough just to reproduce material from the Web in your coursework without further comment. The nature of the Web is that anyone with web access can post anything they like on it, whether it is accurate or not. Nor is the Web a stable information environment. Web addresses are constantly changing, so that what appeared at a particular URL one day may have shifted to a new address by the next. Netiquette suggests that a link to the new address should be left at the old address for a little time, but this is not always adhered to. Information at one address may change from time to time or even day to day as the webmasters (not always male please note) update their sites.

You therefore need to ask yourself a series of questions about any web-derived information in order to deploy it effectively in your project.

1   The first set of questions relates to the poster of information:

- What or who is the source of this information?

- Is the source a reputable one?

- Is the source an organisation or an individual?

- If the source is an organisation, what is its status – a publicly funded body such as a university or a private organisation with a particular axe to grind?

- If the source is an individual, how credible is the information being posted?

- Is the source of the information likely to lead to bias?

- How reliable is the source of information?

2   The second set of questions relates to the content of the information:

- Is the information presented, balanced in its approach?

- Is there an in-depth treatment of the subject, or is it a superficial approach?

- Does the information present a valid picture of the issue?

- Are there any obvious omissions from the content?

- Is the use of language unbiased?

- Is the information corroborated (confirmed) by other sources you have read or seen?

- Is the language used accessible to you?

3   The third set of questions relates to the use to which the information is to be put:

- How does this information relate to my project as a whole?

- Does this information support or refute my hypothesis?

- In which sections of my coursework will I use this information?

- What words will I use to connect the information to my project when I introduce it?

- How can I apply this information to points I make in my context?

- How sociological is the information?

- What criticisms of the information can I make to show evaluation?

These questions are important, because without them you may be tempted to use the information in an uncritical way. Coursework demands a whole range of skills, some of them quite sophisticated. It is important then to show the marker that you are using information from the web in a sensitive manner, being aware of the dangers in using information from such an open medium. On the other hand, used thoughtfully as a source of up-to-date and extensive information, the WWW is an unparalleled boon to the sociologist engaged in coursework.

Access to the WWW also allows you to be creative in the types of evidence that you can include in your coursework. As broadband connections to the Internet become more common, the amount of digital information that can be placed quickly onto your computer increases. This means that the information available to you is not just written texts. Many websites now incorporate a whole range of multi-media presentations to enhance the message which they wish to put across. Sound files and graphic images are commonplace, and increasingly, video clips and three dimensional presentations are being included. To access these, your computer system needs extra software, which is often provided free as 'plug-in' applications. You just follow the instructions on the screen to download such software onto your hard disk. However, you do need plenty of memory to capture all of these applications and if you are using the school's facilities you should check to see what is available or request those free applications which you think might be useful. There is nothing to stop you submitting a computer disk with video clips or graphic images to support your A2 coursework – especially if you are doing a project in the area of the media itself.

17.5 Communicating with others using the Internet

The opportunity to surf the Web is not the only use you can make of the connection to the Internet. The truly innovative feature of the Internet is that you can communicate with others regardless of time or distance. You can do this in a number of ways, as described next.

E-mail

The most usual way of communicating with others using the internet is through e-mail. Schools and colleges have different policies over providing students with an e-mail address. Your e-mail address is a unique designation through which you can send and receive messages. An e-mail address might look like this:

<tzl22@le.ac.uk>

The address after the @ shows where the computer is located; the part before the @ is your specific designation. The main advantage of e-mail is its speed, but for coursework purposes, there are several other advantages:

* You may want to send messages to other students who are interested in the same area of research as you. If you know their e-mail addresses you can start a 'conversation' with them. You can also try to contact other sociology students in schools and colleges using the e-mail facilities found on the Web pages of many schools. A general request for a contact can often prompt a reply from students interested in your area of research.

* Some experts on specific sociological issues are happy to receive messages from students and will try to answer their queries. You can usually find the addresses of these sympathetic academics at certain websites (more on this later).

* You can choose to e-mail your research respondents a questionnaire, asking them to fill it in and return it to you electronically. This often works best when you are using students from your own school or college, where you may have access to a distribution list of their e-mail addresses (a record of all the e-mail addresses in each year of the school, for example). This saves you having to send an e-mail to each respondent individually. You might also improve your response rates as people tend to respond more readily to e-mail messages.

* If you know the e-mail addresses of students in other areas of the country, you could work collaboratively on your coursework. For example, you could devise a questionnaire on a topic to be given to respondents in each location. The information gathered could then be sent electronically, as a file attachment to an e-mail to each of the collaborators. This would allow students to carry out a comparative analysis of an issue rather than be confined to one geographical location. Or you can arrange to swap information with students from other schools or colleges, such as their institution's examination results or ethnic make-up.

Mailing lists

You can also gain access to experts and others in a particular field of study through appropriate mailing lists. These are groups of like-minded individuals who subscribe to a mailing list based around a particular topic. You can e-mail requests for information or contribute to e-mail discussion by sending your message to a particular web address from where your message is then distributed to all the members of the mailing list. There are various ways in which you can find out about mailing lists and how to subscribe to them. You can look on the Web at: <http://www.mailbase.ac.uk>, or put 'mailing lists' into a suitable search engine.

The problem with a mailing list is that you will receive all the messages that subscribers submit and not just the ones which are pertinent to your request. You will have to wade through a lot of messages and there is no guarantee that any will be of use to you. You may also gain access to the archive of a particular mailing list, which will let you examine previous correspondence about a particular issue. However, you may encounter the common problem of 'information overload'.

You should also remember that, as these are open forums for discussion, it is easy to offend other participants if you are not careful with the way you express yourself. There are netiquette conventions available from the net itself to help you avoid being 'flamed'–that is, attacked electronically. Remember, however, that it is even more important that you ask yourself the questions about source, content and use, which we identified in section 17.4. Subscribers to a mailing list are self-selected and it may contain all sorts of individuals, not just sociologists. It is also important to be aware of conventions concerning physically meeting those to whom you are introduced via the Internet. The general rule is that you should not arrange any meeting with electronic contacts under any circumstances. This is for your own protection.

Electronic conferencing

A more focused way of communicating through electronic means is by closed and/or video conferencing. With closed conferencing, you could interview/correspond with those respondents who are geographically distant, if you both have access to the same conferencing software, (such as FirstClass). This ensures that such conferencing is protected from anyone else joining in by passwords. This means that you are more likely to communicate with only those who will be helpful to you and, in the spirit of co-operation which pervades the Net, be helpful to others as well.

Even more 'state-of-the-art' is video-conferencing software such as CUSeeMe, which allows you to communicate face-to-face, regardless of distance. Though this takes some time to organise and depends on all participants having video-conferencing software, it does provide you with the most realistic possibility of interviewing others who are not from your geographical area. It could thus provide you with a rich source of data contrasting to those which you collect locally.

Bulletin boards

If you have the appropriate software, you can access public domain bulletin boards, where you can post messages on the topics that interest you and respond to those who share that interest. You can also read messages that others leave there. Many of the boards are free, but some require subscription. You also have to be aware of the unsuitability of some of the messages that can be posted. Remember the golden rule—you should never arrange a meeting with someone whom you have only met electronically. The Internet provides users with the opportunity to create their own user identities thanks to its 'virtuality'. This can be negative as well as positive, in that the motives of those who use bulletin boards may not always be pure. So be responsible in the way you approach them.

UseNets

UseNets are collections (often of many hundreds) of newsgroups (subscribers interested in a particular area), which require newsreader software to access. If you wish to use the information contained in newsgroup archives and current listings, you should go to an educational UseNet in the first instance, as these are more likely to provide you with reliable information. There are several things to note about UseNets. Firstly, read the frequently asked questions (FAQs) section before you start posting questions of your own. A lot of the information you require may already be there. Secondly, when you first access a newsgroup, 'lurk' for a while, that is, observe without comment. This will allow you to get used to the netiquette of your newsgroup so you will not annoy the others. Lastly, not all ISPs will give access to UseNet and you will need to find out whether your school's/college's provider does. UseNet usage is also subject to your institution's AUP and you should only access suitable newsgroups.

17.6 Managing and tracking the collection of information and data

Action planning

One of the difficulties you will face when doing your coursework is finding ways to manage your time appropriately. While you are focused on your sociology coursework, there will be plenty of distractions, such as the other subjects you are studying, their coursework demands, your duties and responsibilities at home and of course the small matter of a social life! While there may seem to be plenty of time in hand to carry out your coursework, you will soon find time slipping away and the last thing you want is to get within two weeks of your deadline and find you have not yet done your actual research. So, you need a system which will allow you to plan when you are going to do particular activities and record when and how you have achieved them.

Both awarding bodies require a research diary to be kept and submitted with the main A2 coursework. Though it is not formally assessed, it is a way of showing the marker that you have followed through a proper research process when planning and delivering your project. Electronic diaries and planners are now widely available and should help you to form an action plan for your research.

Your action plan should divide the process of research into sections such as planning, reading, doing interviews, analysing data, writing up, etc. (see pages 124–127). Each of these sections should be allocated a particular length of time, always keeping in mind the final deadline and other demands that may be made on you. The advantage of an electronic planner is that you can use it as a flexible document, changing your plans as unforeseen circumstances interfere with the flow of your research. You can be assured that there are all sorts of problems which will delay your project–organisations that do not respond quickly to letters and requests, problems with finding a sample, etc. By planning out your scheme of research on an electronic planner, you will be able to adjust your timings as needs dictate and see the consequences for the subsequent timings of each section of your research. With a fixed end-date (your coursework deadline) the effect of problems is nearly always to squeeze your timings, and a planner will show you how this affects each remaining section.

A
B
C
D
E
F
G
H
I
J
K
L
M
N
O
P
Q
R
S
T
U
V
W
X
Y
Z

Referencing systems

In one specific part of your research, ICT can be helpful for managing your data and that is the necessary reading for the sociological context of your particular project. To be successful, you will need to place your research questions into the sociological literature that addresses the problem you are interested in. To help you identify the important pieces of sociological books that you will use and reference, you could use a referencing system of recording. An example of such a system is EndNote, which allows you to create your own card index on the screen. The advantage of EndNote is that, as part of the Microsoft suite of applications, it can create automatic references in your coursework file. For books, each Endnote entry should have the title of the book, the author(s) names, the year of publication, the publishers and space for notes. If you are using articles (and many students use articles from *Sociology Review* for their context), then the title of the article, author(s) name, journal, year of publication and volume and issue number should be recorded. These are the details you will need if you are going to use any information from a book in your project, as you will have to reference the source in your bibliography (see 13.5 Writing up the project).

Reference type: Book
Record number: 2
Author: Garrod, J., Clynch, A. and Lawson, T.
Year: 1999
Title: A-Z Sociology Coursework Handbook
Series editor: Marcousé, Ian
Series title: The Complete A-Z Handbooks
City: London
Publisher: Hodder & Stoughton
Number of pages: 180
Edition: First
ISBN: 0 340 74919 9
Keywords: dictionary, concepts, coursework, ICT
Notes: This contains everything you need to know about doing your sociology coursework. It has advice sections on resources for coursework and a section on using ICT to assist coursework.

Figure 17.3 An example of an EndNote entry

You should also have space on each entry for notes taken from the book or article (see Figure 17.3). This restricted space should encourage you to take down only the most relevant details, so that you need to keep the focus of your research always in mind when you are taking notes. You can, of course, do all this on paper cards if your school or college does not have the software, but it is the search facility of EndNote that will be most helpful to you. When you have completed all your research notes, you can search your 'stack' (all the entries which you have written notes on) for particular terms or concepts. This will allow you to bring together all the information about a specific term or idea and gain a thorough understanding of the way that different sociologists have approached it. So, if you think you have read somewhere about a particular concept, but cannot remember where, rather than searching through all your notes looking for that term, EndNote allows you to 'find' the concept at the click of a mouse. This enables you to manipulate your information in relatively sophisticated ways.

17.7 Recording and analysing your data

There are now many sophisticated applications available for creating research instruments and analysing sociological data once it has been collected. There are systems which will help you to design your questionnaire or interview, carry out complex quantitative analysis and statistical functions–for example the Sphinx Survey from Scolari. There are systems which allow you to carry out complex analysis of interview data, such as QSR's NUD*IST. However, regardless of whether your school or college has access to these, they are really designed for professional researchers and not for AS/A2 students. By the time you have learned rudimentary ways of using these systems, your coursework deadline is likely to have passed! Moreover, you are unlikely to have a sample which is large enough for any statistical analysis of your data to be formally conclusive. Such systems are therefore just too sophisticated for your present needs. However, that does not mean you cannot use ICT applications to help record and analyse data.

Creating research instruments

Which ICT application you use to create your research instrument depends on the method you have chosen. If you have decided that unstructured interviews or questionnaires are the best way of collecting the information you need, then a straightforward wordprocessing application is all that will be necessary.

You can create a template (a design to be used with all your interviewees/respondents) which will allow you to gather all the variables you need and give space for respondents to answer open-ended questions about the issues that interest you (see Figure 17.4 for an example).

Interview on Examination Achievement

Name ....

Gender ....

Age ....

Question 1
How many GCSE passes (A–C) did you obtain?
(Please state which subjects)

Question 2
How many other GCSEs (D–G) did you obtain?
(Please state which subjects)

Question 3
What was your favourite subject at GCSE and why was it your favourite?

Question 4
What is your opinion of the teaching you received in your favourite GCSE subject?

Thank you for your cooperation in this short questionnaire.

Figure 17.4 An example of a questionnaire

If, however, you are going to use more structured interviews or questionnaires, (perhaps because you wish to generate more quantifiable data), then you will be able to get a more precise layout of your questions by using a drawing package such as ClarisDraw, or a specific application for designing forms such as Smartform Designer. Although most of the recent wordprocessing packages allow you to create boxes for ticking and so on, specialist drawing applications allow you to be much more precise in where you place your text and boxes and how you arrange your questions. They are very easy to use, as long as you remember that you need different tools for the various effects you wish to create. The tools menu is usually found at the top of your screen. So, if you wish to write text you need the writing tool which is often signified by a capital A. For drawing boxes you need the tool which looks like a box, and so on (see Figure 17.5 for an example).

Questionnaire on Educational Achievement

Name

Gender   Male   Female
(please circle
 appropriate choice)

Please indicate the number of GCSEs (A–C) you obtained by ticking in the appropriate box

0 GCSEs (A–C)

1 GCSE (A–C)

2–5 GCSEs (A–C)

6–7 GCSEs (A–C)

8+ GCSEs (A–C)

Thank you for your cooperation in completing this questionnaire.

Figure 17.5 An example of a designed questionnaire

You might also wish to extend the principle of using a specific application to design your research instrument if you are considering an observational study. Sociologists often use tick charts (sometimes called tally charts) when carrying out observations so that they can quickly generate quantifiable data from observing specific events. For example, if you were observing a GCSE classroom for differential male and female student behaviour, you might design a tick chart which allows you to put down different types of behaviour for identified males or females during five minute blocks. An example of just such a tick chart is shown in Figure 17.6. Here the different types of behaviour

Tally Chart for Observations of GCSE Classroom

Subject being taught

Date   Year

Teacher   Male   Female

Target observed   Male   Female

Name of observer

Type of behaviour

	1	2	3	4	5	6	7
5 minutes							
5–10 minutes							
10–15 minutes							
15–20 minutes							
20–25 minutes							
25–30 minutes							

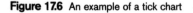

Figure 17.6 An example of a tick chart

are indicated by numbers, so that the observer can assign relevant behaviours to each column. Behaviours might be 'asking question', 'answering question' 'listening' 'not listening', etc.

Recording using spreadsheets

Where your research has been structured, either through the collection of information through a questionnaire or in a structured interview, most spreadsheet applications will provide a useful way of recording information and carrying out simple correlations and analysis. The most popular spreadsheet for this type of work is probably Microsoft Excel, because not only is it simple to learn and operate, but it is also linked to an integral graphics package, which allows you to translate your findings into effective graphs, bar charts and the like (see Section 17.8).

A spreadsheet is a large squared area, made up of columns down the screen and rows across the screen. These form cells, into which information may be placed (see Figure 17.7). This information may be text, numbers or formulae. The usefulness of a spreadsheet in analysing your data lies in the way you can arrange the answers to your structured questionnaire or interview to generate percentages and display the results. If you are intending to use spreadsheets in this way, it is likely that you will use closed questions rather than open-ended ones, as they are easier to codify and turn into numbers. The important thing to remember here is that you should not allow your desire to use spreadsheets to determine the kind of questionnaire or interview you develop. Start by deciding what type of information you need to explore your hypothesis/research questions properly. If you decide that information expressed numerically will help you to test your hypothesis then a spreadsheet might be of use. However, if you decide that your research questions need rich, qualitative data, then a spreadsheet will be less useful.

	A	B	C	D
1		Column		
2		Column		
3	This is a cell	Column		
4		Column		
5		Column		
6		Column		
7	Row	Row Column	Row	This is a row
8		This is a column		

Figure 17.7 Cells, rows and columns in a spread-sheet

The organisation of your spreadsheet should be kept as simple as possible, but needs to be related directly to the questionnaires you send out. For example, for 20 respondents replying to a simple questionnaire regarding gender and educational achievement, you could set up the spreadsheet shown in Figure 17.8.

Using this form respondents' answers are likely to result in information which can be expressed as a number. For example, asking whether a respondent is male or female can result in only two responses. This can be recorded on your spreadsheet as a positive number (1) for the category indicated and a neutral number (0) otherwise. Similarly, if a respondent indicates 6–7 GCSEs for their educational achievement, a 1 can be placed in the appropriate cell.

	A	B	C	D
1		Respondent 1	Respondents 2	...Respondent 20
2	Males	1	0	0
3	Females	0	1	1
4				
5	0 GCSEs (A-C)	0	0	0
6	1 GCSE (A-C)	0	0	0
7	2-5 GCSEs (A-C)	1	0	1
8	6-7 GCSEs (A-C)	0	1	0
9	8+ GCSEs (A-C)	0	0	0

Figure 17.8 A spread-sheet for use with a questionnaire

Calculating using spreadsheets

When you have collected all 20 respondent's replies, you can use a formula to express the information as a total number or as a percentage. To remind you what these numbers or percentages refer to it is usual to keep them in the same rows as your data. This may involve you in scrolling across the screen to get to the formula cells. A formula for a percentage of males where there are twenty respondents would be =sum(B2:B22)/20*100. All you are doing here is asking the spreadsheet to count the number of 1s in the range of cells indicated (B2 to B22 in this case, the range being indicated by the colon), divide it (/) by the number of respondents (20) and multiply (*) by 100 to give a percentage. The equals sign tells the spreadsheet that this is a formula. You would then do the same for females, except the cells would be a different range (in this example, C2:C22). You can use the same principle to generate cross-tabulations (simple expressions of the connections between variables) by organising your rows and columns in slightly different ways. For example, you can use gender as your column headings and educational achievement as your row headings. In the example just described, you need to put in the total number of females with the particular number of GCSEs in the appropriate cell and then do the same for males, as in Figure 17.9.

	Female	Percentage (females)	Percentage (males)	Male
0 GCSEs (A-C)	2	20	10	1
1 GCSE (A-C)	2	20	20	2
2-5 GCSEs (A-C)	1	10	20	2
6-7 GCSEs (A-C)	5	50	50	5
8+ GCSEs (A-C)	1	10	0	0

Figure 17.9 A spread-sheet for use with a questionnaire

The formula to generate the percentages here is different because you only want to calculate the percentage of females with one GCSE, etc. Here we would therefore use: =**sum**(B12)/10*100, where B12 refers to the cell you want to make into a percentage and where you only have a population of ten females (rather than all your respondents).

It may be that you are quite confident in calculating percentages yourself, using a calculator, and you find it easier to go through the questionnaire or interview returns by hand, counting the appropriate cases of females with no GCSEs, males with two to five GCSEs, and so on. This is absolutely fine. The most important lesson in information technology is to know when it is best to use it, and when it would be simpler and more time-saving not to do so. However, if you are a worried about your calculating abilities, then a spreadsheet might be the answer. You must however, be careful to ensure that your formulae actually calculate what you are intending them to. For example, one common mistake is to use the wrong figure for your population. If you have 20 responses, but only ten from females, you need to remember that in calculating any percentage of female responses, you need to divide by ten and not 20. If you have any doubts about what you are doing, it is perfectly legitimate to ask your teacher if your formulae are correct, as long as you request that he or she tells you only whether they are right or wrong. If they are wrong then you yourself need to work out where you have gone wrong and make the necessary corrections.

Analysing using spreadsheets (pivot tables)

Pivot tables can be found in Microsoft Excel's later versions and are an easy way to to help you think about the data you have collected and how you might best represent them in graphical forms. Pivot tables combine a simple way of working out cross-tabulations and other statistical relationships with the sophisticated graphics facilities of Excel. Once your raw data are placed on the spreadsheet, the crucial decision you have to make is which bits of the data you want to analyse using the pivot table. You will need to highlight the data you are interested in and then go to the 'Data' command at the top of the screen and choose 'Pivot Table' from the options.

The rest is very easy, as you are taken through the steps, one by one, by a progam called a Wizard. It is mainly a matter of clicking on the variables you want to analyse, dragging them to the appropriate position to achieve a cross-tabulation, or some other statistical calculation such as sum, count or average. When you have finished your pivot table, it can be displayed wherever you choose on your original spreadsheet. You can then use the graphics facility to transform your analysis into an appropriate chart. Pivot tables are so easy that you can play around with different ways of cross-tabulating and analysing data, even using trial and error as a way of experimenting with your figures. The important thing to keep in mind is what your pivot tables are showing you in terms of your original hypothesis or idea, and using only those that have some bearing on it.

Even if you end up calculating your percentages and cross-tabulations without the aid of the spreadsheet, you might want to consider placing the final results onto one. This is because you can use the spreadsheet to turn your figures or percentages into a whole range of graphs, bar charts, pie charts and the like. It is to the issue of presentation that we will now turn.

17.8 Presenting your project

Graphics

Electronic spreadsheets are usually linked to graphical presentation packages, so that whether you are using secondary or primary numerical data, you should consider placing the raw data on a spreadsheet to produce illustrative charts and graphs. However, there is a golden rule to consider if you decide to use a graphical package to illustrate data:

A pretty picture is no substitute for thought.

You should not assume that presenting information in the form of colourful graphs and charts is all you need to do by way of analysing your data. On the contrary, graphs and charts are only any good if they are:

* **appropriate**

* **clear**

* **analysed.**

1 Appropriateness

To be appropriate, you need to consider what it is your data is representing and how that might be best illustrated in a chart or graph. If you want to compare two categories, such as male and female, then a bar chart is probably the most useful diagram. First, you need to arrange your numbers in such a way that the desired comparison results from the conversion into a bar chart. The most common mistake here is to miss out a row or column, between your variable names ('male' or 'female') and the percentages (or numbers) associated with those variables. Spreadsheets tend to assume that numerical data is associated only with text which is **directly** adjacent to it. You should then use the click and drag function of your mouse to highlight the information you wish to convert into a bar chart. Be careful that you do not cover too many rows and columns, because the spreadsheet will assume that these are zero entries, rather than ignore them.

You then need to go to the command which allows you to convert raw data into a diagram ('Gallery' in the case of Excel) and choose the most effective type of bar chart for a direct comparison of male and female responses (see Figure 17.10). One of the things you will find is that, if you have only a limited number of responses, the bar chart may not be very informative when it is produced, as the differences between the variables may be small. You will therefore have to decide whether it is worth including the chart in your project at all. The crucial, deciding factor should be the relationship of the comparison to your hypothesis or research questions. Remember that 'no difference between males and females' might be an important finding for your particular research question.

If you are interested in any changes over time which your raw data may indicate, then converting that information into a graph might be the most appropriate thing to do. Looking at how the number of males and females gaining six to seven GCSEs has changed over the last ten years might be best done with a graph (see Figure 17.11).

Note that you can use colour to highlight the difference between categories

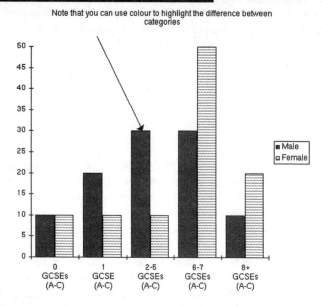

Figure 17.10 A bar chart, showing male and female responses

If you are however interested in the distribution of something (such as the different proportions of females who gain 0, 1, 2–5, 6–7, or more than 8 GCSEs in any one year) a pie chart might be more suitable (see Figure 17.12). For a pie chart to be successful, you need your total figures to add up to 100% of the cases you have recorded. You can of course use pie charts to show differences over time or between genders, by producing two or more pie charts.

2 Clarity

In the case of clarity, there are several devices available on a spreadsheet package which allow you to illustrate clearly what you intend. With colour printers now widely available, you should consider the use of colour to distinguish between the important component elements of your graph or chart. You will probably need to seek permission to use a colour printer from your school or college, as they are more expensive to use than ordinary black-only printers. It is also a good idea to use the colour printer only for your last copy, to prevent waste. If you do not have access to colour, then you can use hatchings (patterns of black lines and dots) to distinguish your components.

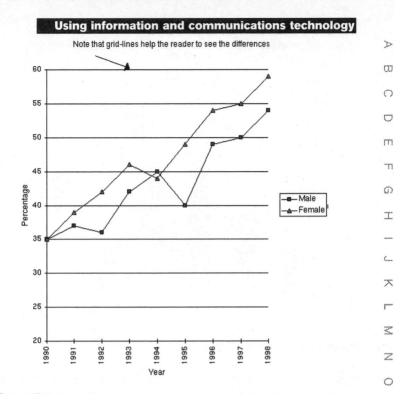

Figure 17.11 A graph showing data over a ten-year period

Colour and hatchings may be used together, but be careful that the result is not so fussy that it obscures, rather than illuminates, the data. If you use either of these features you should ensure that you have included a key (sometimes called a legend) which explains what each of the colours or hatchings represents. You might also add grid-lines to a diagram to help the reader access the information more easily.

Labelling of your chart or graph is essential. You can achieve this through a key, but most spreadsheets will seek to attach the elements automatically to their appropriate labels. If the spreadsheet needs some help there are facilities for you to add your own labels to elements of your graph or chart. You can also add explanatory text and arrows to draw attention to the most important findings contained in a graph or chart. Every diagram needs a title to identify what it is showing the reader. If you are using secondary data, you will need to add the source of the material under the title.

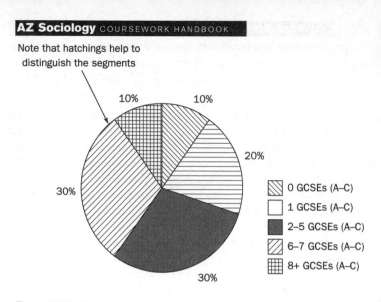

Note that hatchings help to distinguish the segments

Figure 17.12 How to show distribution with a pie chart

3 Analysis

Once you have generated your colourful and informative diagrams, the hard work begins. It is not enough to just throw in a large number of diagrams in the hope that they will somehow speak for themselves. You need to show the marker that there is some purpose behind the inclusion of those diagrams, in that they are supportive or critical of your research question or hypothesis. You should therefore view the purpose of spreadsheets, not as 'prettifying your project', but as a way of getting you to think about the significance of the data you have collected or taken from other sources, in the framework of your rationale and hypothesis.

You need to analyse the features which your diagram demonstrate, because in so doing you will be showing the marker the AO2 skills of interpretation, identification, analysis and evaluation which are an important component of the mark schemes for coursework. You must avoid the temptation to reproduce only the statistical information in the charts, with no other commentary attached to it. For example, if all you do with Figure 17.12 is to write that 30 per cent of males achieved two to five GCSEs (A–C) in 1998 you are just reiterating what the diagram shows. The only skill you are demonstrating is the ability to repeat. You can begin to analyse your diagrams by interpreting what the figures might mean. For example, you might write about Figure 17.10 in terms of the different patterns that the bar chart shows, such as males achieving a lower number of GCSEs (A–C) than the females from the sample.

To gain further marks, you can show the skill of identification, by using the information contained in the diagrams to address the issues raised in your original aim, hypothesis or research questions. For example, if your hypothesis had been that the gap between male and female achievement at GCSE (A–C) had widened since 1990, then the information contained in Figure 17.11 needs to be used to address this question directly, for example, by stating that there was an identical percentage in 1990 of males and females, but that by 1998 females were achieving more than males by some five per cent. But for maximum impact, the information in your diagrams should be used in an evaluative way, that is, you should show whether the information supports or undermines your original hypothesis or aim. The information contained in Figure 17.11 would support your hypothesis, but you should note that there had not been a constant increase in the gap. In making evaluative statements from your diagrams, you must be careful not to overstate the case. If your primary research included, for example, only 20 respondents, the significance and generalizability of any findings will be limited. You need to place the evaluations you make in the context of the other evidence you have found in the sociological literature and with an awareness of the limitations which are inherent in any A2 sociology project.

In conclusion, if your diagrams are appropriate, clear and analysed carefully, you are more likely to gain high marks. You need to ensure that you think carefully about how you are going to present your findings and then, more importantly, what you are going to do with them. Here are some simple questions you might ask yourself as a checklist of whether you are on the right track:

- **Do the diagrams actually show what the title says they do?**

- **Would someone who has never seen the diagrams before understand what they show? (Give them to a friend to test this.)**

- **Have I attached an explanation of the information to every diagram I am including in my project?**

- **Are the important parts of each diagram highlighted in some way?**

- **Have I related the information in every diagram to my original aim or hypothesis?**

- Have I shown how each important bit of information supports or undermines my original hypothesis?

- Have I included a section on the limitations of the information shown in the diagrams?

- Are there any diagrams included in my project which do not add to my argument? (If there are, get rid of them.)

And remember the golden rule–a picture is not a substitute for thought!

Wordprocessing

The main way in which students use ICT to assist them in their coursework is by wordprocessing it. There is however, no requirement that your project should be wordprocessed nor are any marks given for professional presentation. However, using a word processing package does have advantages over a hand-written approach, both in terms of the process of doing your project and in the product. The most obvious advantage is legibility. If your handwriting is poor, a wordprocessed document will help the marker to read your work. You will not however be penalised by writing your report even if your handwriting is poor. Markers are instructed to make every effort to read examination material regardless of the quality of the handwriting. Nevertheless, you do not want your marker to struggle to understand what you are trying to say, not because you are expressing yourself poorly, but just because you do not write tidily.

The other great advantage of wordprocessing is the ease of drafting and re-drafting your work. You are likely to go through several stages of this process as new ideas and ways of looking at things come to you through the process of doing coursework, or if you need to reduce the number of words. Your coursework should be a journey of discovery about a particular issue and so you will need to add to and alter your text as you go along. Through the processes of cutting, copying and pasting, you can manipulate the text of your coursework to the best advantage. For example, if late on in your project you come across a sociological text which is very useful, you will be able to insert important insights from it into your own work at appropriate points without completely re-writing the report.

A facility that you may find particularly useful here is Revisions (or Tracking Changes in earlier versions of Word). This is usually found under 'Tools' in the main menu, and allows you to suggest changes to text without committing yourself fully. The original text is retained, crossed out in a different colour, with the amended text alongside. You may then return to each alteration in turn and make a decision about whether you want to keep it or not. If you are unsure, you might have someone else, (like your teacher) look at the alternatives, always remembering that there are limits to what is acceptable help.

Wordprocessing packages are now very sophisticated and have many other features which may prove useful to you as you construct your final text. Most packages now have the ability to embed graphical material amongst the text, so that you can place your diagrams into appropriate spots in the flow of your discourse. Note however that once embedded, it is sometimes difficult to alter the diagrams, unless you have a fairly sophisticated wordprocessing package. As OLE (object linking and embedding) facilities in wordprocessing packages become more common, you will be able to change your diagrams within your project document more easily. However, if you do not have the facility or choose not to incorporate your diagrams into your text, you can still refer to them in the main body of your work and use a graphics package to generate the actual diagrams.

Other features that are important when you are wordprocessing a relatively long document are:

* **spell checking**
* **page numbering and word count**
* **table of contents**
* **footnotes and endnotes.**

1 Spell checking

This is one of the last things that you should do, but remember using the spell-check facility of a word processing application does not guarantee that you will have a correctly spelled document. If, for example, you mistakenly type in 'form' instead of 'from', this will not be picked up. So, it is advisable always to read your document carefully for spelling errors before you print the final copy.

2 Page numbering and word count

This should be the second last thing that you do before printing your final copy of the project (generating a table of contents will be the last thing). Numbering

A B C D E F G H I J K L M N O P Q R S T U V W X Y Z

the pages helps the marker to keep track of your project (it is actually a requirement for both the AQA AS and A2 project) and gives them some idea of the length. Be careful however, that you do not confuse the reader by inserting pages of diagrams from other applications into the wordprocessed text, thus throwing the page numbering into confusion. You will need to include a word count with your project. This is very easy to do with a word processor, using the Tools option. For the AQA AS project, you are required to place the total word count on the title page, and also the word count for each of the four sections at the end of each section. To calculate the word count for a section of your project, highlight the section and then click Tools on the main menu. Next click Word count. For the AQA A2 project, all that is required is the total number of words, excluding appendices and bibliography, to be placed on the title page. However, as both OCR and AQA have recommendations for the length of sections as well as the total project, using the word count facility will enable you to keep control of the structure of your project and assess whether you are on target.

3 Table of contents

By marking the important headings in your coursework (rationale, context, methodology, etc.) using the Table of Contents facility, you will generate an automatic table of contents with page numbers. This is a requirement for both the AQA and OCR A2 specifications. Do not forget to include any appendices and your bibliography in your table of contents.

4 Endnotes and footnotes

This facility enables you to reference the sociological works you are referring to without interrupting the flow of text. Most wordprocessors have an automatic footnote/endnote numbering system, so that even if you insert one into your text later, the rest are automatically re-numbered correctly.

5 Other features of use

Other features of wordprocessing applications may be of use in more creative ways. If your wordprocessing application permits you to use colour for your text, you should consider doing this as a way of identifying where you have employed the stated skills. For example, when you have a nearly finished version of your coursework ready, go through it and change the colour of the text in all the places where you think you have shown interpretation skills. Do the same for analysis and evaluation, using a different colour. If you can print off a colour version of your project, do so and then ask yourself if there are any opportunities you have missed to demonstrate these important skills. Look at the amount of each of the skills domains you have highlighted using the different colours, and see if you need to do some more work on them. The text of the final version should, of course, be just in black.

You also need to pay some attention to the design of your project document, for example considering which font to use, what size to have the text, how to show headings and sub-headings. While these decisions are often a matter of taste, there are some principles of good design which you should consider when producing your document:

- **your font should be of a size which makes it easy to read for the average reader. In most cases, this will be 12 point or above**

- **you should always leave a space between paragraphs. Use either the Return, or the paragraph spacing facility**

- **while the font you choose should be one that you like, it is not good practice to put several different fonts into the same document. At the most you should only have two (possibly one for the main text, one for quotations if they are extensive)**

- **underlining does not work well in wordprocessed documents, so consider emboldening headings and sub-headings**

- **headings and sub-headings should be distinguished by size and boldness; headings of equal status should appear in the same size and format throughout the project**

- **use italics and indents sparingly – usually just for long quotations, book titles and foreign words**

- **decide on a convention for emphasising words (bold or italic) and stick with it throughout.**

In conclusion, it is worth remembering that ICT is only a tool which can assist or hinder you in your coursework. The worst thing that could happen is that you spend so much time trying to work out how to do things on the computer that you forget to think about the sociology you are doing. There are no marks for ICT in coursework projects. So, why consider using ICT?

Mainly because it is a very useful tool. Using a wordprocessor allows easy alteration of your project document as you add more sociology or better data to it. This will save you time in the long run but more importantly allow you to get the report right. Using ICT gives you access to a wealth of information, up-to-date and pertinent, which would otherwise be very hard to access easily. It will also help to make your project look good, so that the points you wish to make and the data you wish to use are clearly put across to your readers (of which the most important is the marker). ICT can help you if you are not very confident in manipulating numbers; this is one of the key skills in all AS/A2 level courses. Having to organise your material to produce the appropriate statistics will assist you in understanding how numbers work. Used carefully and thoughtfully, ICT will provide you with the means to produce an effective AS or A2 sociology project and provide evidence that you have reached a key skill standard for ICT appropriate to advanced level study.

A–Z glossary of sociology coursework

Acceptable Use Policy (AUP): a statement by your school or college as to what are legitimate ways of accesing the Internet. The AUP is designed to prevent deliberate access to unsuitable Internet sites and to stop flippant usage that costs the institution money. Before you use the Internet to gain information for your project, make sure that you are familiar with the rules laid down by the institution (or the responsible adults) who pay for your access.

action planning: a process whereby you can plot your way through your coursework using a combination of targets, strategies and timings. The principle behind action planning is to break down a large project into more manageable tasks. You set yourself small-scale targets, related to the stages you have to go through in order to finish your coursework by the deadline your teacher gives you. For example, 'collecting information from existing literature on the topic of your coursework' might be an appropriate target. You then identify the strategies which need to be followed to achieve the target (search the Resource Centre, access the Internet, etc.) and give yourself a time by which you have to achieve the target. The timings are related to an overall action plan, which lays down in order the steps you have to take to finish your coursework, and the time you are allotting to different stages. Note that action planning is meant to be a flexible process, allowing you to meet unforeseen circumstances by adapting strategies and targets.

aims: in coursework, aims are related to the *rationale* for the study, that is, a clear statement of the reasons for carrying out your study. The aims should not just be restricted to the section on your rationale, but should be referred to in any conclusions and evaluation of your study.

analysis: this is where you seek to explain your findings to the reader. It involves taking information that you have discovered, either from other *sources* or from your *primary methods*, and demonstrating what it means, both in itself and in terms of your *hypotheses* or *aims*. Analysis is part of the *AO2* assessment objectives in both AQA and OCR specifications. It is therefore very important that you demonstrate analytical skills in your project.

annexe: in the OCR specification, this contains all the raw data that has been gathered, for example from questionnaires, tape or video recordings or *interview transcripts*. This type of material may be placed in *appendices* in the AQA specification.

annotation: the process whereby you write on *interview transcripts* to draw out the significance and importance of what your interviewees have said. Annotations should therefore be related to your original *hypotheses* or *aims* and should assist you in analysing your data. You might consider using a coloured pen to annotate your transcripts, as this will help you when you refer back to them.

Annual Abstract of Statistics: a yearly government publication, which identifies key statistical data collected by officials on social and economic issues. Published by the Stationery Office, it is a rich source of recent findings from a number of government departments and thus an invaluable tool for coursework.

anonymity: the principle that participants in social research have the right to privacy, so that, without an express permission to include names, all data collected in your coursework should be unattributable (that is, information cannot be traced back to any individual). This is an important dimension of the code of ethical practice for sociologists engaged in empirical research and is particularly important where sensitive or controversial issues are being investigated. The guarantee of anonymity will also help your *response rate*.

anthropologically strange: a sociological concept that refers to the ability to see the ordinary and everyday as if it were a strange and exotic culture. This is part of the *sociological imagination* and is an important skill for sociologists to acquire. When you are carrying out your project you should try to not take anything for granted, but look with fresh eyes on what seems natural in your world. This is a difficult thing to do, but is part of the creative process of sociology.

AO1: the assessment objective that tests the sociological knowledge and understanding of candidates. It also includes the ability of candidates to communicate their knowledge effectively.

AO2: the assessment objective that tests the skills of identification, analysis, interpretation and evaluation.

AO weightings are the percentage of the marks given in coursework to *AO1* and *AO2* assessment objectives. In the AQA specification for the AS coursework option, AO1 contributes 7.5 per cent and AO2 contributes 7.5 per cent to the total A2 mark. For the A2 coursework option, AO1 gives 6 per cent and AO2 gives 9 per cent to the final A2 total. There is thus a greater emphasis on AO2 in the A2 coursework option. For the OCR specification, AS coursework contributes 8 per cent from AO1 and 7 per cent from AO2 to the final A2 total. The A2 coursework has 7 per cent from AO1 and 8 per cent from AO2 towards the A2 total. Again, there is a slight shift towards AO2 in the A2 coursework option.

appendices: these are additions to the main coursework study, they usually consist of material which would interrupt the flow of the argument if they were contained in the main body. In the OCR A2 specification, the Appendix has to include the proposal for the study, a single copy of any questionnaires, or interviews, and single examples of letters sent to other people or organisations and their responses. In the AQA A2 specification, the Appendix should include one page of the *research diary*.

assertions: claims which are not supported by any evidence or facts. In social research, assertion must be avoided and you should therefore seek to provide supporting evidence for any claims you make in your project. Assertions are often associated with stereotypical commonsense statements and are therefore the opposite of sociological statements, which should always be based on the careful weighing of the evidence in favour of and against any specific claim to truth.

attitude scales: though most often used by social psychologists, the use of a numerical measure of individual attitudes has its place in sociological coursework also. Most frequently used in experiments or structured questionnaires, attitude scales are an attempt to measure the depth of feelings or attitudes towards a particular issue by giving respondents a choice of responses along a numerical scale. They often look like this:

Please circle the number that corresponds most closely to your opinion about the following statement:
'The House of Lords should be abolished immediately'

1	2	3	4	5
Strongly agree	Agree	Don't know /Don't care	Disagree	Strongly disagree

One of the advantages claimed for attitude scales is that they allow for a statistical analysis of responses and give a more textured set of results than simple agree/disagree measures.

attitudes: predispositions to look at issues in a particular way, which are held over a period of time and which are fairly stable. Sociologists are interested in the attitudes that people have on topics and they are often the object of sociological research. Many coursework students choose to investigate the attitudes of their respondents in some way. The problem is that the research is reliant on the subjective statements of the respondents regarding their attitudes, as these have no tangible existence. You cannot see or measure one exactly. You can only measure what the holder says about their attitudes.

autobiographies: a way of collecting information from individuals by asking them to write down or relate their life story. You are unlikely to have the time in your coursework to explore autobiography as a methodology, as it takes time to find and persuade individuals significant to your topic to write down their life stories. As individuals will take their own time to write their story there are no guarantees that they will be completed before your deadlines. However, you may wish to explore a limited version of autobiographies, in asking identified individuals to write down specific parts of their life history, such as their experiences when they started their A Level course, etc. An advantage of an autobiography is that you would be allowing participants to speak for themselves in their own words. Disadvantages are that they may forget or not tell the whole truth. For this reason, autobiographies are usually triangulated with other sources of information.

authentication statement: this is a signed declaration by the candidate that the work is their own, rather than anyone else's, such as parents or previous candidates. This does not include legitimate assistance given by the candidate's teacher. For the AQA, this declaration should be included on the Candidate Record Form (CRF) (see also *guidance*).

behaviour: the actions of individuals or groups which have a tangible existence, that is they can be observed by sociologists as an objective reality, whenever people do things. Behaviour is often studied through various observational techniques. However, the intentions of the people exhibiting the behaviour are subject to the subjective interpretation of the observer, or the vocal expression of the person doing the behaviour.

beliefs: ideas which we think are true and which therefore inform and shape our behaviour. Like attitudes, they can only be accessed through the expression of the holder of the belief and are therefore subjective. This means that, if you choose to investigate people's beliefs, you must be careful what you say about them. You must also know that individuals often hold what seem to be contradictory beliefs and that they may not always fully know themselves what their beliefs are.

bias: a 'wandering' from the truth due to distortion from a number of possible sources. Bias in your coursework can appear in several different ways:

- **it may be that your method of sampling introduces some systematic bias into your work, such as inadvertently including an unrepresentative proportion of one particular religious group if you were exploring issues of morality – this bias towards a particular religious group might mean that your findings were not truly representative of the population as a whole**

- **bias might also intrude into the questions you ask, leading your respondents into one particular answer when it may not be what they actually believe**

- **the self-interest of your respondents might also be a source of bias and you need to take account of this when interviewing your sample – the views of teachers about what happens in a classroom, for example, are likely to be biased by their particular role there**

- **bias may also appear in your analysis of your findings as the temptation here is to interpret the results of your study in the way most favourable to your existing beliefs – this appears most often in coursework as the desire to find that your hypothesis is confirmed.**

Dealing with bias in your coursework is not easy and it would be very difficult to eliminate it completely. The best you can do is to be aware of bias as an issue, seek to minimise it where you can and discuss the possible biases in your work in your evaluation of the project.

bibliography: the list of books, articles, newspapers, magazines, Websites, etc. which you have referred to in the main body of your project. It is a requirement of both the AQA and the OCR specifications. There are different conventions as to the proper way to reference. Which one you choose is less important than sticking to the same one all the way through.

black: a variable often used in coursework questionnaires or interviews to identify one type of ethnic origin. It is a wide-ranging concept, covering Afro-Caribbeans, Africans, Indians, Pakistanis, etc. and for that reason is often seen as a blunt measurement of ethnicity. However, it does have its uses when a contrast with those of 'white ethnic origin' is being sought.

British Sociological Association: the major professional organisation for British sociologists and the source of the Code of Practice for ethical research to which you should adhere.

case study: a detailed investigation of one person, one group or a specific event, which provides the sociologist with rich descriptions as a source of data. Case studies can stand alone, in the sense that you could carry out the whole of your project just using a case study approach. However, in sociological research with more resources, case studies are often used for *triangulation* with other research techniques, to investigate phenomena in more depth. Case studies are therefore important because they are a source of *validity*, enabling exploration of the complexity of social phenomena.

category: a grouping together of similar phenomena into one classification which assists sociologists in interpreting social life. For example, ethnic groups might be categorised in different ways, such as black, white, South Asian, etc., in order to explore the differences and similarities between the different categories. Categories provide you with the most basic units of sociological research in your coursework.

causal explanation: a relationship between phenomena in which the existence of one element is accounted for through its creation by the other elements. In sociology overall, it is difficult to establish accurately the causes of phenomena, not least because humans have free will and can change the conditions under which things might be caused. It is unlikely that you will be able to establish causal relationships with the limited time and resources that you have in your coursework. However, you should be able to provide supporting or conflicting evidence for causes established by professional sociologists.

choice of method: the process whereby a researcher decides upon the technique(s) which she or he will employ in investigating a particular issue. The factors that influence the choice of method are many and include the topic under consideration, the type of data required (qualitative or quantitative), previous research findings, the *practical constraints* and ethical considerations. You will need to examine all these factors when you are deciding on the techniques you are going to use in your coursework.

closed question: a multiple-choice or fixed choice question, where *respondents* have to choose between pre-determined categories of response to questions. Closed questions are often used to ascertain the *social characteristics* of respondents as in the following example:

Are you male or female? Please tick the appropriate box:

Male ☐   Female ☐

cluster sampling: most often used in market research, this refers to choosing respondents from a relatively small area (geographically or socially) because they represent a particular segment of society, important for your research. In many A Level projects, a cluster sample is taken from the school or college itself, because many students choose to investigate some aspect of schooling and their peers represent a convenient cluster of students (see also *convenience sampling*).

coding: where the researcher attaches numbers to respondents' questionnaire answers, in order to carry out statistical processes upon them. Coding is used especially with closed questions, but may also be used where the answers to open-ended questions fall into similar categories. If you are confident with statistics and have enough respondents to make it worthwhile, you should consider coding. Even where you have a limited number of responses, attaching numbers to responses can help you analyse the answers.

cohort analysis: using generation as an organising principle, this is research into groups which have a similar age profile, or share some other feature in common. Many coursework students choose some form of cohort analysis as they select their peers in school or college to investigate. The reason for this is that the cohort of 16–19 year olds is a convenient one to investigate, and often constitute a captive audience.

comparative method: the classic sociological method in which two or more societies, organisations, locations or whatever are compared with each other to establish how they are similar and how different. Usually employing statistical measures, (though not always), the aim is to establish how these differences or similarities came about and whether there are any generalisations which can be drawn from them to apply to all other similar phenomena. A good piece of research might engage in some form of comparative method, even if it is at the level of the classroom, school, localities, etc. (see also *quasi-experimental method*).

concept: a short-hand term which stands for more complex realities, and used by sociologists as convenient descriptions of social phenomena. There are many concepts which are used by sociologists in their research, such as gender, social class, ethnicity, etc. and one of the hall-marks of a good piece of coursework is the ability to utilise relevant concepts in natural and effective ways, so that the text reads as a sociological discourse.

A B C D E F G H I J K L M N O P Q R S T U V W X Y Z

confidentiality: the principle that all information collected during your project should remain private, that is individuals should not have their answers to questions or their behaviour during observations discussed in a public and attributable way. This means for example that you must let no one but yourself have access to your *raw data* and if you are including any examples of questionnaires, etc. in your final project, all names or means of identification should be removed.

constructs: this is used to refer to *concepts* or ideas which can help the sociologist understand the social world, but which are also abstract and therefore constructed by someone as an explanatory aid. The term 'social class' is a construct because it helps sociologists to order the social world into groups, but it is not a natural phenomenon.

content analysis: the investigation of some text (written or visual) through the categorisation and comparison of the material under study to generate ideas about the meaning and impact of the text. This is a popular technique used by coursework students, because the media, where it is most often employed, form a favoured area of study. However, it is important that content analysis is undertaken in a systematic way and that the boundaries of the investigation (how long it will be carried out, which texts will be investigated, etc.) are set out strictly to limit the scope of the investigation. Content analysis is therefore not just a question of looking at the material and telling the reader what you think it is saying. The crucial word here is *analysis*.

contents list: one of the front pages of your final coursework that identifies the divisions/chapters in your project and the page numbers where they start. It is a requirement of the OCR and AQA A2 specification and is referred to as the Contents Page by the AQA. It is therefore one of the last things you will do before handing in your work to your teacher.

context: one of the sections of the AQA coursework specification which refers to the theoretical and empirical material which lies at the heart of the issue you are investigating in your project. It is always a good idea to have both theoretical and empirical context.

control group: in an e*xperiment*, this is one half of the participants, who have nothing done to them by the experimenter. They exist as a comparison with the *experimental group* so that any differences between the two groups after the *independent variable* has been manipulated can be seen as a consequence of changes in the independent variable.

convenience sampling: this is to take respondents from the nearest convenient population and in coursework nearly always consists of the students in your school or college. Because this is not a randomly selected sample, it cannot be representative and may therefore introduce bias into your findings. You should take account of this possible source of distortion when you are writing up your project.

conversational analysis: the investigation of speech acts to uncover the rules that govern everyday conversation. When done carefully, conversational analysis can demonstrate the different ways in which men and women engage in speech with each other, or the commonsense rules which allow interruption to take place and so on. The technique is usually associated with the tape recording of speech acts, their subsequent *transcription* and then careful *analysis*. This makes it quite a time-consuming type of research, but one that can be very rewarding for the coursework student.

correlation: a link between two or more *variables*, which is usually expressed in a numerical form. A classic case of a correlation would be the incidence (amount of) lung cancer in society and the proportion of the population who smoke cigarettes. You need to be careful not to make assertions about causes just from correlations. While it may seem as if changes in one variable lead to changes in a second, this does not prove that there is a causal relationship between them. You are likely to make good use of correlations if you choose to do a questionnaire for your project. Relating one variable to another is the way that sociologists seek to analyse the information they collect. For example, if you were investigating the variation between males and females (the gender variable) in GCSE performance (the achievement variable) you would establish any correlations between gender and achievement and express them in the form of tables.

corroboration: where evidence from one source is supported by evidence from another. It is a good idea to seek corroboration of information, especially where it comes from only one informant, such as in *diaries*.

coursework: a general term used to describe work undertaken individually by students during a course of study. The AQA specification calls 'coursework' projects that are carried out by a student partly in their own time and on a topic of interest to them (see also *personal study*).

cover sheet: the AQA A2 specification requires this, with the title, student name and number, centre name and number and word count.

covert participant observation: a technique in which the sociologist takes part in the activities of the group under study, without their knowledge of his or her status as an investigator. The idea is to try and achieve an untainted understanding of the way people live their lives. However, it may be that the mere presence of another person may change the dynamics of the group under study. Covert participant observation has some potential for a coursework technique, but you will find that there are difficulties with it due to the limited amount of time you will be able to spend with a group. Some students choose to study a group they are already a member of, but do not tell their colleagues that they have added a role and so accelerate the process of participant observation.

covert research: where the investigator is either hidden from view or their role as a sociologist is unknown to the subjects of the study. The hidden nature of covert research is to allow access to social life as it is lived, without the dangers of the *Hawthorne effect*. It is possible to carry out covert research in your project, but you must consider the ethical issues if you do so.

cross-sectional studies: research which captures a single moment in time and therefore provides the sociologist with information about a specific time only. Most A Level research is likely to be cross-sectional because of the severe restrictions in time with which you are faced. However, it is possible within the time limits to carry out two cross-sectional studies and use them as a basis for comparison (see also *longitudinal studies*).

cross-tabulations: a way of analysing quantitative data which seeks to compare variables by placing them against other statistical information. For example, if you were interested in the differential incidence of smoking amongst males and females in your school, you might represent your findings in a cross-tabulation such as:

Gender	Percentage of smokers
Male	24
Female	30

data: the raw material of your coursework, these are information, expressed either numerically or verbally. It is your data that you will analyse in the light of your research questions or *hypothesis*.

decoding: a reading of media messages, which seeks to unravel the encoded messages placed in the text by the originator. Many coursework students choose to decode the images placed in the media as part of their project. The problem with decoding is to convince others that your interpretation of the message is a valid one.

deconstruction: one way of reading texts (visual or written) to demonstrate their ultimate ambiguity. By deconstructing texts, the sociologist seeks to show that meanings are dependent upon the privileging or devaluing of interpretations by social institutions. Though this is a difficult skill for A Level students to accomplish, some coursework students do attempt this successfully, as long as they are careful to show exactly how they are operating.

deep meaning: used in *semiology* to indicate an implied or less literal interpretation of a sign or symbol. For example, a simple white flag flown in certain contexts can symbolise surrender at a deeper level of meaning.

dependent variable: in an *experiment*, the factor that changes as a consequence of the manipulation of the *independent variable*. The differences in the dependent variable between the *experimental groups* and *control groups* are measured to establish what effect the manipulation of the independent variable has had.

depth interview: a series of open-ended questions spoken to an interviewee by an interviewer, which explores in detail a specific topic. This common technique attempts to expose the rich, complex nature of phenomena and to establish meanings and intentions through a delicate but deep probing of a small number of *key informants*. One of the problems is that depth interviews take so much time that interviewees may be reluctant to commit to the project, or the researcher can only carry out a limited number of them.

diaries: documents which try to record the events of individual lives, as they happen (that is, contemporaneously). They can either be pre-existing, in which case they will be difficult to access as most people are reluctant to allow you to see their most personal thoughts, or generated, that is, you can request informants to keep a diary of their life for a short period of time. You can even ask them to focus on particular issues.

direct observation is where the behaviour being investigated is watched by the sociologist her/himself. The sociologist can therefore form a view of the behaviour from their own observations (see also *indirect observation*).

disrupting normalcy: a research technique, associated with *ethno-methodology*, where the researcher deliberately challenges taken-for-granted rules of behaviour in a particular circumstance to study the response of other participants. A classic example would be to sit next to somebody on a near-empty bus. Such a technique is illuminating but raises many ethical issues concerning the discomfort other participants might feel.

documentary analysis: reading papers and publications in order to tease out meanings and explanations which are not always immediately obvious through a surface reading. Documents can be many things in A Level research including sociological works themselves, and they can all be subject to a careful and detailed reading to try and get beneath the surface appearance of the text.

domain assumptions: the pre-existing 'truths' that you take for granted and which you therefore bring into your coursework, often without even knowing it. They often take the form of partial perspectives, where you approach an issue from a particular point of view and with some ideas already half-formed about an issue. It is actually very difficult to identify your own domain assumptions about an issue, precisely because they are often subconscious. However, it is a good idea to try and write down what you already think about the issue you are going to study, before you start your project. In this way, you can audit your domain assumptions and look back on them at the end of the project to help you in your evaluation.

ecological validity: where the characteristics of the population as a whole can be correctly attributed to groups within the population. In your coursework, you must be careful that you do not make assumptions about groups based on information about the whole population. For example, if you were looking at your school, you cannot 'read off' the characteristics of a single class from the profile of the whole school.

electoral register: one of the main *sampling frames* used by sociologists. If you are engaged in research about a local community then the electoral register is one of the main ways you can access individuals to involve in your study. However, remember that it does have limitations, for example excluding those under 17 and those who do not register.

e-mails can be used directly as *sources* of evidence. For example, the history of e-mails between two *key informants* would tell a story about their inter-relationship. In an age where formal letter writing is disappearing, e-mails may constitute a new form of *evidence*.

empathy: the ability to place yourself in another's place and understand the social world from their point of view. The ability to empathise is a key sociological skill for coursework as you have to be able to understand other people's positions if you are going to exercise your *sociological imagination*.

empirical studies: research which includes the collection of *data* and facts as opposed to the generation of ideas alone. Because of the limited time available to coursework students, most choose to engage in some form of empirical research. However, it is possible to do a project that focuses on ideas and theories without engaging in direct empirical research.

epoché: the ability to put the world in brackets, so that the mundane and everyday becomes open to a new interpretation by treating it as if you were approaching it for the first time. You will need to examine familiar circumstances with fresh eyes if you do your coursework on aspects of social life with which you are personally engaged.

erklären: literally explanation, this is associated with a scientific way of doing research and seeking explanations for social phenomena (see also *hypothetico-deductive method*).

ethical constraints: these are the limits you have to place on your project so as not to harm, upset or be untrue to other people. There is a fine line between using a technique legitimately to discover information that could not otherwise be found out, and unacceptable behaviour. Be sure that you read the ethical guidelines provided before you plan your research strategy.

ethnic groups: categories of people mainly distinguished by a common culture, language and history. Such groups would be for example, the Irish, Bangladeshis or Roma. Though often associated with national states, ethnic groups sometimes transcend these.

ethnocentric: ideas and issues seen from the particular point of view associated with a person's cultural and social background. One of the main criticisms which is levelled at sociological research is that the values of the investigator will intrude into the research, and create a biased view, often from a specific cultural stance. You need to be aware of the potential for ethnocentricity in your own project and take care not to let the assumptions which you already hold influence the way you see things (see also *objectivity*).

ethnographic studies: research into the culture or way of life of a group through direct *observation*. Though there are obvious limits of time and opportunity in carrying out an ethnographic study in a coursework project, you may be able to do a limited ethnography of a group to whom you are already connected, such as a youth club or your classmates. You need to be aware however, of issues of *ethical constraints* if you decide to do ethnography.

ethnomethodology is a *perspective* which stresses the constant ambiguity of social life, in which all interactions are a struggle for meaning.

evaluation: a required section for all pieces of coursework, as well as one of the skills on which you will be marked. Evaluation has two meanings for projects. Firstly, you should be evaluative in the way that you judge arguments, debates and evidence, weighing up the pros and cons of what you have found in your research so that you come to a balanced conclusion. Secondly, you have to be evaluative about your own performance as a researcher, looking at how you have carried out the research and identifying the ways in which you might improve it if you had to do it again.

evidence: all the facts and figures, arguments and documentation which you bring to bear on the issue under discussion. It is on the basis of the evidence that you can come to a particular conclusion. It is therefore important that you organise your evidence in a logical way, so that opposing views or contradictory facts are separated out and that you then come to a conclusion on the basis of the balance of the evidence you have presented. Remember, conclusions come from the evidence.

experiment: a technique normally associated with natural science, it has been used in sociology in different ways and can be seen as a controlled way of investigating social phenomena. The classic experiments are carried out in a laboratory, and the participants are subject to control except in one variable. Any changes in the participants' behaviour as a result of the change can be seen as caused by that change. Because of the ethical and practical problems of carrying out social research in a laboratory, many sociologists have turned to *field experiments* as a way of replicating the laboratory experiment. In your coursework, using a laboratory experiment is one way of limiting the amount of research that you have to do, while keeping a very focused approach (see also *dependent variable* and *independent variable*).

experimental group: in an *experiment*, this is one half of the participants, who have something (the *independent variable*) done to them to measure the effects of the change on them (see also *dependent variable*).

experimental method: see *hypothetico-deductive method*.

external moderation: this is where A2 coursework, marked by your teacher, will be checked by the AQA examiners to see if the standardised marks have been given to it. There is no external moderation for OCR A2 candidates as all marking is done by Awarding Body-appointed examiners and not by your teacher.

external validity is the potential for the findings of your research to be generalised to a wider population. It is unlikely, given the number of respondents you are able to use within the time and resources available, that any AS/A level coursework project will establish external validity (see also *internal validity*).

extrapolations: where you push forward an idea or trend into the future on the basis of past performance. Extrapolations can be statistical. This is where you look at the changes in the statistics over recent years, identify the trend and then carry it through to the future, like this:

Year	2000	2003	2006	2009	2012
Number of Smokers in Knighton School	250	200	150	100	50

Extrapolations can also be non-statistical, for example looking at social trends and drawing conclusions about the likely shape of society in the future. While the evidence that you collect during any primary research is unlikely to allow you to extrapolate statistically, there are *secondary data* projects that would allow some form of extrapolation into the future – for example if you were interested in the social effects of information and communications technologies.

falsification: where sociologists try to prove their *hypothesis* wrong through testing it to destruction. The idea behind this is that it is relatively easy to pick out evidence that supports your hypothesis and ignore that which disproves it. Therefore by designing tests which seek to disprove the hypothesis, you avoid accusations of *bias*. Though few students choose the strategy of falsification in their coursework, you must be prepared to accept that your hypothesis may be shown to be false by your data, and always keep this possibility in mind (see also *verifiability*).

field experiment: a controlled investigation carried out in social situations rather than the laboratory. If you are creative enough you may be able to set up a field experiment which might illuminate the rules of everyday life (see also *disrupting normalcy*).

fieldwork: another name for general research carried out in the social world rather than the laboratory. Most coursework students will engage directly in some form of fieldwork during the course of their investigations.

footnotes: explanatory text which is placed at the bottom of a page and identified in the main text by means of a number. Footnotes are used to explain further the meaning of concepts or technical terms, when placing

A
B
C
D
E
F
G
H
I
J
K
L
M
N
O
P
Q
R
S
T
U
V
W
X
Y
Z

them in the main text would interrupt the flow of the argument. Most word-processing packages now have automatic footnoting facilities.

formal interviews: asking a series of questions face-to-face, but in a way which will be less chatty and relaxing than an *informal interview*. The aim is to gather as much standardised information as possible and convey the seriousness of the interview to the interviewee.

frame of reference: a particular way of looking at the world drawn from an individual's experience. You need to be careful not to allow your frame of reference to colour what you see and so introduce *bias* into your coursework.

function: the job that an activity or institution performs for society as a whole. If you are approaching your research from a functionalist point of view or are critical of *functionalism*, you may make a great deal of use of this concept.

functionalism: a perspective which stresses social order and the inter-relationship of elements of society. It is the starting point for much sociological research, including A Level coursework.

funding: the resources needed to carry out sociological research. Although you will not need formal funding for your coursework, you should recognise that there are costs involved in items like photocopying, etc. and you need to take these into account when you are *action planning* your research.

gender: one of the key *variables* of sociological research, this refers to the social roles associated with being a male or a female. Many coursework projects are focused on the differences and similarities between males and females in social life.

generalisation: statements about a *sample* of individuals which can be applied to all those with similar characteristics. Generalisability is based on having sufficient *sample size* to have the confidence to use the findings of your study with larger but similar groups in society. As you will be restricted in time and money, your ability to generalise is likely to be limited. However, you may, for example, be able to make generalisations about the population of your school or college on the basis of a sample of students from it, as long as that sample is large enough.

generalised other: the ability to take the place of other people and calculate the effects of your actions upon them. You need to take the place of the generalised other when you are deciding on which research technique to use, so that you gauge what effect your choice will have on those on whom you do your research.

generation: another key variable in sociological research, this is the age groupings in society usually defined by a span of 30 years. For example, you belong to a different generation from your parents.

glossary: a list of words and their accompanying explanations usually placed in an appendix at the end of the project. There is no requirement to include a glossary and it is unnecessary to explain commonly used sociological concepts. However, if your project concerns an area of social life that may be unfamiliar to the marker then it may be wise to include one. For example, if you were looking at a particular industry in which technical terms were used, then a glossary might assist the marker.

glossing: the ability to ignore possible misunderstandings in conversation and fill in the meaning of ambiguous phrases. This is one danger in interviewing, that is, that you do not take the real meaning of the interviewee but gloss a meaning that you want them to have.

going native: one of the dangers of *participant observation* in research is that the researcher takes on board the view-points of those observed in their entirety and thus loses *objectivity*. If you engage in any form of participation in your project, you must be wary about losing your sociological focus.

group: a number of individuals who interact regularly because of some formal or informal connection between them. Many coursework projects are concerned with groups and the way that they interact.

guidance: the legitimate support given by teachers to their coursework students. As a basic rule-of-thumb, teachers can offer advice on the candidate's proposals and monitor their progress, but should not seek to correct the final submitted project.

Hall-Jones scale: a standard occupational scale that groups occupations into seven categories, in a hierarchy of prestige. This is one of standard measures of occupational classes and has been much used by sociologists. You should be particularly careful if you are replicating a study which uses occupational scales that you employ the same one when you carry out your investigation.

halo effect: one of the dangers of interviewing is that the *respondent* will give the answer that he or she thinks the interviewer wants. You must be careful if you choose to do interviews that your interviewees are relaxed enough to respond honestly to your questions.

hard statistics: reliable statistics, such as birth, death or marriage statistics, which are usually collected in a systematic fashion by government agencies. They are often the basis for much sociological research and are an important resource for coursework students.

Hawthorne effect: a reaction of the observed to being observed, so that any change in behaviour is the result of the increased attention they are receiving rather than any other reason. The Hawthorne effect is one of the main reasons why researchers often choose *covert methods*.

hermeneutics: a process of analysing events or texts by locating them in their original contexts, so that the background which produced them can also be understood. It is one of the ways that sociologists try to gain an authentic understanding of social phenomena. In many projects, a description of the social context is a good way of helping the reader understand the research being undertaken.

heuristic device: an idea or analogy which helps us to understand complex realities. You may wish to seek out ways of explaining your ideas through heuristic devices, either drawn from the sociological literature, or analogies which you have developed yourself.

high theory: an explanation of the social world which exists at a rarefied and abstract level, with little reference to empirical studies. It is usually associated with complex concepts and many levels of inter-relationships between social elements. While you are unlikely to develop your own high theory, one possible piece of coursework could be to examine the *validity* of a particular high theory.

historical documents: papers from the past which can be helpful in explaining both the particular events which occurred and the reasons why they happened. Historical documents are an important resource for sociologists, because sociologists should seek to place events in their proper historical context.

hypothesis: a statement which is put forward as a possible explanation for a phenomenon, and which is tested to see whether the *evidence* supports it or not. The hypothesis is one of the most important statements in your coursework as it is the linchpin around which you have to devise your research strategy and the measure against which you must check your findings. It is therefore imperative that you give a great deal of thought to developing your hypothesis, because it must be plausible (a realistic possible explanation) and checkable (it can be tested for its truth or otherwise).

hypothetico-deductive method: a process of conducting research in a scientific way; it involves following a set series of stages.

- **observation** – identifying a phenomenon to be investigated and observing it

- **forming an *hypothesis*** – developing a possible explanation for the phenomenon

- **experimentation** – testing the hypothesis through data collection and logical analysis of the results

- **theorising** – confirming or rejecting an hypothesis. If confirmed, then *generalisations* may be made to similar sets of circumstances.

Though this is in many senses an *ideal type* of research, your own coursework is likely to follow this format, with some amendments depending on the area you are studying (see also *logics-in-use* and *reconstructed logics*).

ideal type: a description of a particular aspect of social life which is formed by the extraction of its essential characteristics from numerous real life examples. Ideal types are common in sociology and coursework students can use them as a way of comparing real life examples of a phenomenon with its ideal type.

identity: the established sense of self which an individual develops as they go through life. The forms of identity that many coursework students deal with are *gender* and ethnic identities, though others examine religious or class identities.

ideology: a systematic set of *beliefs* which are the expression of the self-interest of a particular group. You need to be aware of your own ideologies when you are carrying out coursework, so that you do not introduce *bias* into your project by allowing your ideology to affect the way that you carry out your research.

independent variable: the factor that is manipulated during an *experiment* to see what effects it has on the *dependent variables*.

indicators: factors which stand for or point to other more abstract factors, for example, shopping habits may be an indicator of social status. When you are operationalising many social characteristics, you may have to use indicators rather than the thing in itself, which may be too complex for a questionnaire or interview. Most sociologists use occupation as an indicator of class.

indirect observation occurs where the effects of some behaviour are investigated, rather than the behaviour itself. For example, the contents of a waste basket in the student coffee bar after break might be examined for evidence about consumption patterns (see also *direct observation*).

informal interviews: asking a series of questions of an interviewee in a relaxed and open manner. The aim is to create as natural a situation as possible so that the interviewees will open up and give the interviewer detailed and truthful information about themselves.

informants: those who are used as sources of information for a research project. The term is used to describe individuals who have more control over a research event than interviewees traditionally have as passive receivers of questions (see also *key informant*).

information and communications technology: this refers to a whole range of computer-based facilities which can be used to assist you in your coursework. They include word-processing, superhighways access, spreadsheets and databasing.

insight: a flash of inspiration which reveals an understanding of a situation or individual. Many coursework students experience insight when they are carrying out their research as something previously hidden becomes illuminated by the research.

interactionism: a *perspective* which stresses the interactions of individuals as they go about their daily lives. Many projects focus on these types of interactions and how social life is thereby accomplished.

internal validity is the ability of your chosen method to measure what you think you are measuring and not to be confused by other *variables*. It is often associated with the laboratory experiment or the *comparative method* (see also *external validity*).

Internet: as well as a 'library of libraries', it can also be used directly as a source of data. If you are interested in the sociological aspects of Internet content, then a content analysis of websites is an option for you. If you are interested in semiology you could use deconstruction as a technique of analysing some chosen web pages. Remember to conform to your school or college's '*acceptable use policy*'.

interview: a series of questions asked by the researcher directly face-to-face with the *respondent*. There are many different types of interview and you need to consider carefully what type of information you need before you choose one of them (see also *formal interview, informal interview, structured interview and unstructured interview*).

interview schedule: the list of questions which make up one interview and which may be used repeatedly with different respondents.

interview transcripts: verbatim written accounts of interviews which can be used in conjunction with *annotation*. Writing up interviews is an immensely long process and you must be careful to make due allowance for it when you are planning your project. Take care not to let the transcribing of interview tapes substitute for analysing their contents.

interviewer bias: where the *respondent* in an *interview* situation reacts to the social characteristics of the researcher so that inaccurate or biased information is received. It may be a case of hostility to the social characteristics of the researcher or it could be a desire to please the interviewer that leads to the bias. It is important that you seek to minimise interviewer bias if you choose this method and therefore you need to consider whether your ethnic background, gender, age, etc., will intimidate or otherwise affect your respondents.

key informant: an individual who is central to a research project because they are in a position to provide the researcher with most of the important information they need. A key informant is likely to be in a crucial social position in terms of the topic under consideration.

knowledge: a set of *beliefs* which is claimed to be true. Although your aim in your coursework may be to extend the knowledge of sociology you should be careful not to make over-grand claims for the knowledge that you find. It is likely to be partial and limited.

laboratory experiment: see *experiment*.

life-history: an account of a person's life often obtained from them through *unstructured interviews*. You need to treat such accounts with caution because of the inexactitude of memory and the ability of people to put the most favourable interpretation of events for their position into their life-histories.

logics-in-use: this is used to describe the actual way research is carried out rather than the way it is written up, which is subject to formal conventions and *norms*. In your project you need to be aware of the difference between logics-in-use and *reconstructed logics*, so that you can be honest about the way that your own project went.

longitudinal studies: research which is carried out over a long period of time on a continuous basis and which may also involve some comparisons between the beginning and the end. As the time that you have available for a longitudinal study will be limited you are unlikely to choose this method (see also *cross-sectional studies*).

macro sociology: a general term which covers those *perspectives* which start their analysis by looking at society as a whole. These include *Marxism* and *Functionalism*. One of the most common ways in which A Level students engage in some form of macro sociology is by looking at *official statistics*, and/or using the *comparative method*.

mailed questionnaires: see *postal questionnaires*.

malpractice: any questionable activity in coursework which gives an unfair advantage to a candidate, and proof of which can lead to disqualification for the examination. The most common forms of malpractice are *plagiarism* and recycling.

margin of error: the range within which any percentage is likely to fall. It is calculated on the basis of the likely *sampling error* involved in taking a *sample* and is expressed as 'plus or minus X per cent' where x is the calculated margin of error.

Marxism: a *perspective* that stresses social conflict and social class. Once a popular starting point for coursework, it has become less common as other perspectives such as post-modernism or new left realism have taken hold.

mean: the arithmetic average of a distribution. This is one of the most basic calculations you might do if you are engaged in any statistical analysis of your data. It is calculated by adding up all the values (numbers) in your distribution and dividing by the frequency (number of items you have added up).

meaning: the motivations, intentions or beliefs which individuals give to their actions. Much coursework involves trying to expose these meanings through such techniques as *questionnaires* and *interviews*, where the sociologist seeks to prompt *respondents* to make their meanings explicit.

meta-narrative: a theory which attempts to explain the whole of social reality through one formulation. You are unlikely to generate such a meta-narrative in your project! However, many projects do explore and often criticise sociological meta-narratives for being flawed in some way.

methodology: a term which covers both the research technique which you are going to use in your coursework (questionnaire, interview, etc.), and the research strategy (using case studies, social surveys, etc.). Methodologies are often linked to *perspectives* and you need to think about your general approach to sociology (for example, whether you tend towards a conflict or consensus view of society) before you decide upon your methodology.

micro sociology: an approach to the study of social life which encompasses those theories which start their analysis with the everyday actions of individuals. These might include *phenomenology* and *ethno-methodology*.

misrepresentation occurs where the views expressed by respondents are not accurately conveyed to the reader by the sociologist. This happens to a lesser or greater degree because there will always be a gap between the actual views of the respondent and the way that the researcher hears or interprets those views.

models: often analogies which seek to represent social life by a comparison with a more tangible or familiar object or structure. The classic sociological models of society, for example, compare it to an organic body or a machine. These often provide useful starting points for coursework students. However, it is unlikely that you will be able to develop a model of society of your own in the short time you have available for your project. However, you may try to build models of more specific aspects of social life, such as school or the classroom, etc.

multiple methods: see *triangulation*.

multi-stage sampling: a form of *sampling* which reduces a very large *population* to manageable proportions, by *random sampling* different levels of society. For example, a sociologist might begin by random sampling counties, then towns, and then individuals in towns in a three-stage model. You are highly unlikely to be able to engage in this form of multi-stage sampling. However, if your population was your school or college, you could do a random selection of subject, then of classes within those subjects, and then of individuals within those classes. You would need to be able to justify why you have chosen that way of sampling in your final account of your project.

negative correlation: where two elements are statistically related in such a way that change in one element will create a change in the other in the opposite direction. You will most likely come across these correlations in coursework if you are looking at *official statistics* of some description.

new right: a *perspective* in sociology that stresses individual responsibility and social authority. New right ideas have been both supported and criticised by coursework students, especially those who are more attracted by ideas rather than empirical research.

A
B
C
D
E
F
G
H
I
J
K
L
M
N
O
P
Q
R
S
T
U
V
W
X
Y
Z

newspapers: one of the main *sources* of information which is available to you. As sociology is often interested in contemporary developments, it is important that you use the newspapers to search for current information in the topic of your study. However, you must be aware of the dangers of *bias* in the newspapers as they are not sociological documents and do not have the same rules of evidence for statements as those which will apply to your study. So, you must treat information in the newspapers with some caution and be prepared to write about the difficulty of taking newspaper accounts as the truth.

non-response: contacts for *interviews* or *questionnaires* who do not take part in the survey, either because they cannot be contacted or they choose not to do so. It is important that you establish in any survey that your non-respondents are not different in their social characteristics from your respondents.

normative order: the rules of behaviour which operate in a situation, which are taken-for-granted by participants. Some coursework students choose to explore these rules in their projects, to see what the commonsense understandings of everyday life are like.

norms: the rules of social life which define acceptable behaviour in any given situation. You must be careful to follow the norms associated with research techniques, for example, respecting *confidentiality*.

note-taking: transcribing from books or from *primary research*. Note-taking is one of the key skills you will need in your research. Your note-taking from books and other *sources* should be concise and focused only on the research questions you have established to make the maximum use of your time. On the other hand, note-taking in *interviews* should be as full as possible, so that you do not forget important information given to you.

objectives: the small scale targets which you develop and achieve on the way to fulfilling the *aims* of your project. When you break down your coursework into smaller steps, you are in effect setting yourself objectives.

objectivity: the ability to put aside your own opinions and prejudices and approach your coursework with as fair-minded and unbiased a view as possible. Achieving objectivity is very difficult, especially as your views and opinions can often be unstated and even unconscious. For your coursework, you need to examine your thoughts as honestly as you are able and try to identify the *beliefs* you have which might interfere with your objectivity. You might like to categorise the beliefs which could cause you problems as a starting point – for example, religious beliefs, moral attitudes, political opinions, stereotypes that you hold, etc.

observation: a research technique in sociology and other subjects which is an umbrella term for a number of different ways of looking at the subjects of your study. Observation is the prime technique of all scientists, as they must observe effects if they are to be able to establish causes. In sociology, observation is central because we have to examine our subjects as carefully as we can to establish their patterns of behaviour and their culture (see also *covert participant observation*, *overt observation*).

occupational scales: the hierarchial ordering of jobs into a system of higher and lower status, which can then be translated into class positions. These are one of the main research tools of the sociologist, but are also controversial in their own right. There are several different versions of the occupational scales and each has its own virtues and failings. Before you use any of them in your analysis, you should make sure that you understand the strengths and weaknesses of the different types (see also *Registrar-General* and *Hall-Jones scale*).

official documents: papers produced by the government and which represent the views of the formal organs of the state. Coursework students often find that these are very useful resources for identifying a framework for research projects.

official statistics: the numerical descriptions of social phenomena collected by the agents of the state. They cover such *hard statistics* as birth and death statistics and also *soft statistics* such as consumption patterns. They are an invaluable resource for coursework students, as they provide much basic information in a large number of areas investigated by A Level students.

open questions: these are used in *questionnaires* and *interviews* to allow respondents to reply to a question using their own words. An example might be:

> **What do you think about the present government's performance in the field of education?'**

Open questions are most useful when you are trying to elicit the opinions of your respondents rather than factual details about them. A problem with open questions is that they are difficult to code and analyse quantifiably.

opinion polls: formal collections of the ideas of a sample about a specific subject, in order to gauge public opinion in general. They are usually used for political reasons, such as testing out a policy or establishing voting intentions. It is in these areas that they are sometimes used in coursework.

oral history: where individuals are asked to recount verbally the story of their life. It is a technique often used with the older generation, where writing down life-history may be difficult.

other: a term representing marginalised groups in society who are seen as somehow outside of mainstream society. It is used in the consideration of the position of those groups who have been pushed to the margins of society in a negative way, for example the homeless.

overt participant observation: where the sociologist takes part in the activities of the group under study, but has told the group what she or he is doing. Overt participant observation is often undertaken because of the ethical problems of keeping information hidden from those who are being observed, even though the knowledge that they are being studied may alter the behaviour of the target group. Many A Level students use this form of participant observation, either in their part-time work, or in school or college, or even sometimes in organisations they may belong to such as youth groups or religious bodies (see also *Hawthorne effect*).

overt research: where the presence and role of the sociologist is known to those under study. Overt research therefore encompasses such techniques as *questionnaires* and *interviews*, where it is fairly obvious what is going on, through to observational techniques, where it may be only the presence of the clip-board which identifies the sociologist from the others.

panel studies: where a selected group of people are asked their opinions about an issue over a varied number of times in order to chart any changes in view. Though it is difficult to utilise panel studies in the time you have available for A Level coursework a restricted version can be used effectively, especially where the topic under consideration is live and controversial.

paradigm: a shared set of *beliefs* within which believers operate. It is usually associated with belief in a particular *perspective* or view of the world and paradigms are usually hard to break down. You should be careful not to let the established opinion of a paradigm about a sociological topic unduly influence the way you investigate it.

participant observation: a technique where the sociologist engages in the activities of the group involved so that he or she may experience their actual lives as they are lived and thus gain some *insight* into them. It is a technique associated with *verstehen* and can be of a covert or overt nature. This technique can be accomplished during your project, but you should remember that it is usually carried out over a long period of time. As you have limits in the amount of time you can devote to your project, you need to be aware of the resulting limitations (see also *covert participant observation* and *overt participant observation*).

passing: whereby a covert participant observer is accepted as a genuine member of the group by those being observed. This is one of the most important skills in any covert participation as the ability of the sociologist to observe the natural life of the observed group rests on successful passing.

peer group: those who share a common age and/or gender and/or ethnicity and who tend to live a shared life in some ways. The peer group is often a target for coursework, especially those found in schools and colleges, because they are a convenient source of information about a large number of topics.

personal documents: texts such as diaries or life-histories which are produced by individuals for their own purposes. They can be used in coursework to provide a rich source of descriptive detail to support other techniques used.

personal study: the name given to your OCR specification project by the A2 syllabus; it is the equivalent of *coursework*.

perspectives: organised ways of looking at the social world. Specific perspectives are likely to form an important part of your *context*, as they are often the starting points of analysis in many areas of research. Most investigations are informed by one perspective or another and you therefore need to be aware of the main ones and what adherents have had to say about the particular issue in which you are interested.

phenomenology: a *perspective* which stresses the surface appearance of things and not any hidden depths. The emphasis here is on the stock of knowledge which all individuals have and which allows them to operate in the social world as effective agents.

pilot study: the practice run of a *questionnaire* or *interview schedule*. It is highly recommended that you carry out a pilot study before the main event, in order to :

- **eliminate sources of bias in your questions**
- **check the intelligibility of your questions**

- establish whether your questions actually deliver the information you need to check your *hypothesis*

- ensure that the language level is correct for your *respondents*.

plagiarism: using somebody else's work and presenting it as if it was your own. It is against the Code of Ethics for all academic research and if discovered, can lead to a candidate being disbarred from the examination. You must therefore be careful to use properly referenced quotations if you are going to use another sociologist's work, and take care not to copy out of books or articles. Expressing other people's ideas in your own words is not just a question of ethics, it actually makes you think and helps you understand those ideas.

population: see *survey population*.

positive correlation: where two elements are statistically related such that change in one element will create a change in the other in the same direction. For example, an increase in cigarette smoking is accompanied by an increase in the incidence of lung cancer. You will most likely come across these correlations in coursework if you are looking at *official statistics* of some description (see also *negative correlations*).

positivism: an approach to social research which stresses the importance of a scientific framework, in order to convince other people of the truth of findings (see also *hypothetico-deductive method*).

post-feminism: a *perspective* which argues that the experiences of women are varied rather than similar and therefore it is not possible to talk of a single feminist view-point. Rather, post-feminists believe that women (and men) speak with many different voices in a post-modern world and that these voices need to be taken into consideration when writing about the social lives of both women and men. For example, post-feminists suggest that the experiences of black women are not the same as those of white women, and those of lesbian women not the same as heterosexual women. The implication for your coursework could be, for example, that it is very difficult to write as if all women had the same exploitative experiences.

post-modernism: a *perspective* which stresses the fractured nature of present day social reality, where nothing can be held to be true for certain. Post-modernism is a *frame of reference* that interests many coursework students, as they explore their contemporary social lives.

post-structuralism: a *perspective* which stresses the surface reality of social life, rejecting the idea that there are any underlying or hidden causes of reality. It might be best summed up as an approach that argues that 'what you see is what you get' (WYSIWYG).

postal questionnaires: sets of questions which are sent through the mail to the chosen *sample*. While this is a classic technique used by sociologists, there are costs involved, for example in postage, and therefore it tends to have only restricted use in coursework.

primary data: facts and figures which are compiled by the sociologist doing the research. The analysis of primary data is likely to be one of the main tasks you will perform during your project.

primary research: research gathered directly from the subjects themselves by sociologists, through a variety of means. The distinguishing feature of primary research is that it is carried out in the social world itself rather than the information being gathered through a library, resource centre, etc.

probability: in statistics, the mathematical chance of an event happening under specific conditions. Unless you are very confident in your use of statistics and have sufficient amounts of quantitative data, you are unlikely to need to calculate probability. However, if those conditions which allow you to use probability do apply, then it is a useful technique for the sociologist.

probability sampling: used to select a *sample*, so that every individual has a known chance of being selected, according to their *social characteristics*. It is most often used to ensure that certain social characteristics have a particular representation in the final sample and it is therefore the opposite of *random sampling*.

proto-typicality: where the issue chosen to be studied is at the cutting edge of social development, so that any findings may be seen as indicative of future developments in similar areas. Projects which choose proto-typical scenarios are difficult to find amongst A Level coursework, but some students do choose to check the claims of studies which have claimed proto-typicality to test if they are true or not.

qualitative data: facts and findings which are expressed textually as opposed to numerically or statistically. Qualitative data are composed of rich descriptions of social life that illuminate the issue you are investigating. One of the most important research decisions you will make is whether to collect mainly qualitative or quantitative data, or both. Your decision should be linked to the topic you are studying and what you want to find out about it (see also *quantitative data*).

qualitative research methods: this term covers a variety of research methods, where either participants are observed carrying out their daily lives, or where respondents are allowed to speak for themselves. *Participant observation* and *unstructured interviews* are the main qualitative research methods, though you can be equally creative with other techniques (see *quantitative research methods*).

quantitative data: facts or findings which are expressed in a numerical or statistical form. This sort of data is useful for establishing patterns or identifying similarities and differences between phenomena. Quantitative data are preferred by those who adopt a positivistic approach, because numbers are more precise than *qualitative data* and are claimed to be less susceptible to *bias*.

quantitative research methods: this covers a variety of research methods having the distinguishing characteristic that the information they record can be translated into numbers and statistics. The closed questions of a questionnaire or interview are the prime quantitative method (see also *qualitative research methods*).

quasi-experimental method: another name for a form of *comparative* method, which allows the researcher to compare two or more social phenomena statistically to establish differences and similarities. In your coursework, you might engage in this sort of method if you are doing a piece of *secondary research* that involves a comparison of two societies using *official statistics*.

questionnaire: a set of questions, either closed or open, which are given to *respondents* for completion. This is one of the basic tools of the sociological researcher and is favoured by many coursework students.

quota sampling: choosing a *sample* by reference to pre-determined categories which constitute the important *social characteristics* you are interested in. It is often used in market research, but is also a common method of sampling used in A Level coursework. It involves deciding what are the important features of any sample and the proportions you need and then choosing individuals who go together to make up the sample. For example, you might decide that half of your sample must be male and half female, but that there must be 75 per cent under 18 and only 25 per cent over 18. You should then select your respondents to ensure that final result.

random sampling: a specific and important technique of choosing respondents by chance to ensure that the *sample* is representative of the *population*. This is normally achieved using random number tables on a population that has been designated by numbers. While it is good practice to ensure *representativeness* in this way, it is often difficult to do in A Level coursework because the sample sizes are usually relatively small.

rapport: a term used to describe the feelings of well being which may be established between researcher and researched. These feelings lead to confidence on behalf of the researched that the researcher will deal fairly with them and give an accurate account of their lives. It is thus important for getting *respondents* to open up about their lives and attitudes in ways which are useful for your research. It is most important if you choose *depth interviews* as your main technique of research.

rationale: the first section of your A2 research project and, if you are taking the AQA examination, it should include the reason why you have chosen your area of study and your aims and/or *hypothesis* in your chosen field. For the OCR examination, the rationale should also include a description, explanation and justification of your research design and procedures.

realism: an approach which stresses that institutions and structures in society have an existence beyond the lives of the individuals who inhabit them at any moment in time. If you adopt a realist approach in your coursework, you must be careful that you do not fall into the trap of *reification*.

reconstructed logics: the process whereby writing up research is subject to rules of presentation and order. You need to be aware of these rules, which for your project will, by-and-large, be given to you by the specification you are working to, for example the sections which have to appear and the order in which they are arranged. The point is that reconstructed logics do not describe the real process that you went through and you need to be aware of the contradictions in which this may involve you. By being honest about the things that went wrong (and no project is ever perfect) you will gain *evaluation* marks.

recording styles: used to refer to the method of noting down information during research. Issues that you need to consider about your own recording style when doing coursework are: whether to use electronic (tapes, videos etc.) or manual (pen) means of gathering information; when to record (during or after the event); whether the researcher or the *respondent* records the data.

refutation: where an *hypothesis* is disproved through the discovery of a contrary case. This is a tactic that may be used for coursework, as long as you are careful to be open-minded about whether your case study actually disproves your hypothesis rather than engaging in wishful thinking about it. Remember to be modest in your claims to truth.

Registrar-General: though the Registrar-General is an actual person, the R-G's Office is the source of a scale of occupational classes which has long been used by sociologists. Though it has been constantly revised, including a dramatic updating of the number and order of occupational/social class groupings in 1998, much sociological research in the past has relied on the traditional five point scale. Therefore if you wish to carry out a *comparative method* study with already existing findings, you may have to use this scale.

regularities: patterns of activities which can be seen as a routine of everyday life. Much sociological work explores these regularities and A Level coursework is no exception. You are likely to be engaged in researching a pattern of activity in one way or another.

reification: treating abstract concepts such as 'society' as if they were real things which carry out actions – viz, 'society made me do it'. It is very easy to slip into reification when you are carrying out sociological coursework, because we use it so casually in our everyday lives. You need to examine all the statements you make in your project, to ensure that you have not inadvertently reified abstract *concepts* like 'organisations' 'school', 'college', etc.

reliability: when research is carried out in such a strict fashion that another researcher carrying out the same methods in the same way would end up with the same results. Reliability is usually associated with *quantitative methods* and you should strive for reliability if you choose these types of techniques. You should be prepared to document the precise ways in which you have gone about your research so that the marker can come to a judgement about how reliable it is.

replication: the ability to reproduce a research study exactly, in order to check the findings and conclusions of the study. Replication is closely tied to the scientific study of society and is seen as a key feature of the *reliability* of findings. Some coursework students choose to try and replicate published sociological studies, often with interesting results. However, in any evaluation of such a project, you need to be aware that you are unlikely to be able to replicate a study exactly because you will not have the time and money to do so. Therefore, if you choose a replication study, the more straightforward and focused the original study, the nearer a replication you will achieve.

representative sampling: where the subjects of a study have the characteristics of the *population* as a whole from which they are drawn, in terms of the important social characteristics, such as gender, ethnicity, social class, occupation, religious affiliation, marital status, etc. While it is often difficult to gain a representative sample in A Level coursework, because of the restricted numbers involved, where possible you should seek to ensure that your *respondents* do represent the proportions of the central social characteristics which might affect your study.

representativeness: the degree to which the findings of any study about a relatively small number of cases can be said to be transferable to other similar but larger numbers. It is most commonly used in large-scale *social surveys*, where perhaps 1000 or more *respondents* are involved. This is unlikely to happen in your coursework and therefore you need to be careful about any claims to representativeness that you make (see also *generalisation*).

research diary: the day-to-day/week-to-week record which you should keep of the coursework. This is a requirement of both the OCR and AQA A2 specifications. For OCR, the diary has to be submitted with the Personal Study and for AQA, a photocopied page has to be included. It should contain not only your factual achievements, but also your reflections and how you are feeling as you carry out different activities. It is important that you keep a record of your frustrations and failures as much as your successes, as this will help you when you are trying to evaluate your coursework.

research instruments: a concept that refers to the different types of written material which can be used to gather *primary data*. Questionnaire and interview schedules are examples of research instruments, as are *tally charts*.

research proposal: in the OCR specification, the initial proposition submitted by a candidate so that it can be checked for its ethical nature and to ensure that any *personal study* is sufficiently challenging. It should be included in the final submission.

research report: used in the OCR specification to denote the AS coursework task, in which candidates are required to report on some sociological research. It has five sections: source of the research, research objective, outline of methodology, reasons for selection of methodology, outline and evaluation of the findings.

respondents: all those who reply to a request for information as part of a sociological study. Who responds is an important issue for sociologists, because this is related to the *representativeness* and therefore the possible *bias* in your study. In A Level coursework, respondents tend to be located close to the student carrying out the project, as time and money dictates a limited set of respondents. However, some students use e-mail or letters to good effect in gaining respondents from a wider geographical or social area.

response rate: the proportion of your *sample* who agree to take part in your research, either by filling in a questionnaire or agreeing to be interviewed. It is important to get your response rate as high as possible, so that the *representativeness* of your respondents is heightened. The lower your response rate, the more likely that some systematic *bias* might be introduced in the social characteristics of those who are refusing to take part. If you are carrying out a local survey, you are more likely to be able to increase the response rate through a personal appeal. However, you must remember that you cannot force people to take part in your project and they have an absolute right to refuse you.

role: the usual pattern of behaviour carried out by those in specific social circumstances and faced with particular problems or issues. You are likely to make use of this concept at some stage in your research as it is a central idea of sociology.

role conflict: where individuals are faced with contradictory demands upon them. This is a favoured area of research for A Level students, for example exploring the contrary demands on females in work or at school and at home.

role-set: all the roles a person in a particular social position has to adopt in relation to others. This is often the setting for *role conflict* and is a favourite subject for A Level projects.

sample: a small group taken from a larger *population*, which is supposed to represent the whole in some way. Sampling is one of the basic techniques of sociology and you are likely to be involved in it with your project. You will need to think carefully about how you are going to select your sample from your population, depending upon the sample size and degree of *representativeness* that is required.

sample size: used to refer to both the absolute numbers chosen to be investigated from a *population* and the proportion of the population the sample represents. Absolute size is important for your project, because you will be limited in time and money, but you will also need to gather evidence from enough individuals to make the investigation worthwhile. Proportion also needs to be taken into account because it is linked to *representativeness*. The basic rule is that the greater the proportion of a sample, the more representative it is likely to be.

sampling error: a calculable difference between data collected from a whole *population* and the data collected from a *sample* of the population. The sampling error is usually expressed in terms of plus or minus X, where X is calculated from the proportion of the population that is being sampled. The general rule is that the greater the proportion of the population sampled, the more restricted the range of sampling error (e.g. from plus or minus one per cent). Though it is possible to have a large enough sample to calculate sampling error, there are strict conditions under which error can be calculated. If you are going to try and calculate the sampling error, you need to ensure that your technique complies with the principles of *random sampling*.

sampling fraction: the proportion of the population chosen to be investigated. This is usually expressed as '1 in 10', '1 in 3', and so on (see also *sample size*).

sampling frame: the source of the names of the *population* from which your sample is chosen. The most common sociological sampling frame is the electoral register. You are more likely to use a more restricted sampling frame such as the school or college roll.

sampling interval: used in systematic sampling, to select the *sample* from a *population* and usually expressed as '1 in 10' (for a ten per cent sample), '1 in 20' etc. It means that every 10th (or 20th or 30th, etc.) name will be selected from a *sampling frame* as part of the sample.

sampling unit: the level of social phenomena at which selection for a sample takes place. In most A Level coursework the sampling unit will be individuals, because of the restricted time and money available to the average coursework student. Other sampling units might be organisations, such as schools or hospitals, or geographical entities such as towns or villages. You are unlikely to engage with the latter forms of sampling units.

secondary data: facts and figures which have not been produced by the sociologist doing the research, but either by other sociologists, or other agencies such as the government. These are often important resources for coursework students (see also *official statistics*).

secondary research: this is where a project consists of an analysis of already existing findings or materials. In coursework, it might be a re-working of a sociologist's data, or a re-examination of their conclusions. It might also be a book search on a particular topic, looking for all the contributions to a debate or issue. Many sociologists use secondary research when they use *official statistics* to explore a particular sociological issue. There is no assumption in coursework that you have to engage in *primary research*. A secondary research project is just as acceptable.

self-report studies: used often in the sociology of crime and deviance, these are devices to allow individuals to report in confidence and without consequences on their own misdemeanours. This type of *questionnaire* is a popular one amongst A Level students, but it does have its draw-backs such as the probability that not all *respondents* will tell the truth – either hiding their worst offences or exaggerating their involvement in criminality as a show of bravado.

semi-structured interview: sometimes called hierarchically focused interviews, these allow the interviewee to provide information freely, while including specific prompts if the important issues from the interviewer's point of view are not being addressed. Semi-structured interviews are useful where you need to gain both in-depth and standardised information from your interviewees.

semiology: the study of signs or symbols in society. This is usually associated with the study of the media or language and involves the sociologist in deconstructing the messages involved in media events to expose the myths that underlie them.

situatedness: where an individual is located in social formations. You will need to explore the situatedness of any subjects of research if you wish to gain *insight* into their lives and opinions.

snowball sampling: a way of choosing your *sample* by allowing the initial *respondents* to nominate further individuals who might be of interest. Your sample therefore grows as the project proceeds. It is usually used where there would otherwise be difficulties in contacting individuals who have the characteristics you are investigating. One problem is that it cannot be a *random sample*.

social characteristics: the attributable and shared features of individuals which can be classified into specific categories such as gender, ethnicity, class, religious affiliation, etc. They are often used as *variables* in sociological research, so that you may wish to search for patterns of similarity and difference between and within those characteristics. A popular strategy for A Level coursework for example would be to look for differences between males and females in their responses to questions or in their behaviour.

social problem: an area of social life seen as being in need of some remedial action, usually by the government. Much coursework is carried out about social problem issues, for example poverty or crime, though there is no necessity that this must be the case. However, many students are particularly interested in these areas and so choose to investigate them.

social survey: where information is gathered about an issue using some systematic techniques. Because these are usually large-scale it is difficult for a coursework student to get involved directly in a social survey. However, some choose to examine the results of other social surveys in a critical manner and some engage in survey work, but with a much limited population such as a school or college.

Social Trends: an annual document, the highlights of which often appear in the newspapers, which contains a wealth of social statistics. As well as drawing on census returns, *Social Trends* refers to a number of government surveys of the population such as the General Household Survey.

socio-economic groups: broad categories of those who share similar occupations and social status. These are often used in sociological research as important variables in social life, illuminating differences in lifestyle and life chances between different segments of the population.

sociological imagination: coined by C Wright Mills to indicate that it takes creative energy and the ability to transcend everyday life to be a good sociologist. To visualise 'society' and understand social life beyond your own experiences demands that you use your imagination. The hallmark of an excellent piece of coursework is its understanding of the implications of the research carried out for the wider social world.

sociometry: the measurement of relationships between members of small groups using specific questionnaire and observation techniques. Because of its small-scale nature, it can easily be used as a coursework device in exploring the dynamics of groups engaged in particular activities.

soft statistics: numerical measurements of phenomena which are not collected in a reliable manner and which may thus be invalid. Examples might include strike statistics, or church attendance statistics. If you employ these in your coursework you must be aware of the limitations they have (see also *hard statistics*).

sources: this term encompasses the sociological and other work you will refer to during the course of project. A source of information can be many things, from published sociologists' work, through newspapers, academic articles and magazines, to Internet sites and e-mails. From a coursework point of view, you need to take careful note of the details of your sources as you collect them, as it can be very frustrating when writing up if you keep having to break off to find out where you gained some information from.

spurious correlation: where there appears to be a statistical connection between two *variables*, but this is apparent rather than real. It is easy to jump to conclusions about correlations so you need to be certain of your statistics before you make claims for connections that cannot be supported.

standardised interview: *see structured interview*.

stereotyping: where members of a social group are seen in a simplified way as all having the same characteristics. The danger for coursework students is that, because of the limited number of cases they are likely to study, they fall prey to the temptation of stereotyping instead of being cautious with *generalisations*.

stratified sample: a *sample*, in which the population is divided up into appropriate segments according to *social characteristics* before a *random sample* is taken. For example, you might divide your school population into 'white' and 'black' categories and then take a random sample of each. You would then ensure that you had sufficient representation of both categories to make an appropriate comparison.

structured interview: a set of questions asked of the interviewees in the same order and in the same manner. The aim here is to try and standardise the responses as much as possible so that information gathered can be seen as reliable (see also *unstructured interview*).

structured questionnaire: a list of questions given out to *respondents*, in which they are forced to choose between alternative answers (see also *unstructured questionnaire*).

surface meaning is used in *semiology* to indicate the immediate and obvious interpretation of a symbol or sign. For example, a cross on a ballot paper indicates a vote for a certain candidate. It is used as a contrast with *deep meaning*, where, in certain circumstances, a cross also has a deeper, religious meaning.

survey population: the total number of individuals who share the same characteristics and from which a *sample* may be drawn. If for example you wished to have a sample of your school peers, then the survey population would be all the students in your school.

systematic sampling means choosing a sample by targeting for example, every tenth name on a list. It is different from *random sampling* because with systematic sampling not every *sampling unit* has an equal chance of being chosen.

tally chart: also called a *tick chart*, this is a document or *research instrument* which is used to gather systematic observations of people's behaviour. It usually consists of a set number of pre-determined categories of behaviour arranged in columns, against which is a time series (every minute or every five minutes, etc.). The observer's task is to note down the activity being conducted at each time interval so that the systematic patterns of behaviour can be established.

theory: an attempt to explain a social phenomenon systematically and in general terms. Much A Level coursework is concerned with examining theories for their *truth* or otherwise.

third ear: where an interviewer takes into consideration the body language and tone of voice of the interviewees in analysing responses.

tick chart: see *tally chart*.

time budget studies: an analysis of human activities by the recording of the amount of time different activities take in a person's life. They are usually associated with domestic tasks, but they can be applied successfully to many activities by A Level coursework students.

trend: the direction in which a phenomenon is heading. Though trends are usually supported by statistics, they need not be and any coursework student interested in aspects of social change is likely to get involved with identifying trends (see also *extrapolation*).

triangulation: the use of two or more different methods of research to gain different types of information about the subject under study. The opportunities for carrying out triangulation in your project will be limited, but it is a good idea to try and use at least two different methods, if you have time and the subject of your project warrants it (see also *choice of method*).

truth: correct *beliefs*, which have been shown to hold in a variety of situations. While sociologists are engaged in trying to find out the truth of things, the contribution of the A Level student is likely to be at a lower level than this. This should not prevent them however from engaging in correct procedures to try and explore some aspect of society that may be true or not.

A B C D E F G H I J K L M N O P Q R S T U V W X Y Z

unit weighting: this refers to the percentage of the marks that each module contributes to the AS and to the A2 qualifications. For both the AQA and OCR specifications, the AS coursework option contributes 30 per cent of the AS marks and 15 per cent of the A2 marks. The A2 coursework option contributes 15 per cent of the total A2 marks.

universal laws: explanations of phenomena which hold true in every similar situation. While a piece of A Level coursework is unlikely to develop a universal law, some might seek to check the applicability of such a law by looking at specific cases of it.

unobtrusive methods: these are techniques of surveillance or observation, in which the presence of the observer, as observer, is hidden. Unobtrusive means discreet, and the aim of these techniques is to allow the most natural reactions possible by keeping the subjects of the study unaware that they are being studied. However, they do raise ethical issues and if you are planning an unobtrusive method in your coursework, you must gain ethical clearance from your teacher or the Awarding Body beforehand. The main justification for unobtrusive methods is that the information could not be collected in any other way.

unstructured interview: a series of open-ended questions which are spoken to an interviewee by the interviewer. The interviewer is free to follow up any interesting answers with further unwritten questions to pursue avenues of interest (see also *structured interview*).

unstructured questionnaire: a list of questions given to a respondent, which include only open-ended questions. The aim is to allow the *respondents* to answer in their own words so that their voices are heard (see also *structured questionnaires*).

validity: whether the findings of a piece of research describe accurately what it set out to describe. You need to aim for a high degree of validity in your research, whilst recognising that it is likely to be limited in crucial aspects, because you do not have the time or resources to encompass a phenomenon fully.

value judgement: where you make a statement of opinion which is not supported by any evidence that you present. This is one of the ways in which *bias* might intrude into your coursework. You may have such strong opinions (or values) about a particular issue that you want to make a point without having any facts or research findings to back it up. You would not be showing good *evaluation* skills if you let this happen. However, there is nothing wrong with having strong opinions about issues as long as you are open-minded enough to acknowledge that you could be mistaken, if the evidence points to a different conclusion.

value-freedom: the ability to put your own values and *beliefs* to one side while you are conducting sociological research. Though very hard to do in practice, you should make every attempt to suspend your beliefs and values, especially when you are investigating something controversial. At the very least, you should be prepared to declare any strongly-held values you may have about the topic of your research.

variable: a feature which can be measured in some way and which can therefore be expressed numerically. The most likely variables you will use in your coursework are social class, gender or ethnicity.

verbatim reporting is where the responses of a participant are recorded word for word. This is usually achieved by some electronic means (see *recording styles*). The advantage is that the researcher is able to access the full text of a respondent whenever desired. The problem is that the words still have to be interpreted by the researcher.

verifiability: the ability to confirm some *hypothesis*, statement or *causal relationship* as true in certain conditions. It is usually used in reference to the verification of an hypothesis. In the case of A Level coursework, as well as seeking to verify their own hypotheses, many students choose to carry out a replication of an existing study to verify or falsify it. That is, as far as is possible within the physical and other constraints of an A Level project, they test out the truth or otherwise of other sociologists' work. If you decide to do this, you must be careful to measure what you say about professional sociologists' work very carefully, as you are unlikely to be able to reproduce the conditions under which they did their study exactly (see also *falsification*).

verstehen: the ability to put yourself in another person's shoes and see the world as they see it. It literally means 'understanding', but this is a fundamental ability of the creative sociologist. It is this willingness to put aside our own world-view and see the social world from a different angle which is important for developing a rich understanding of the sheer variety of experience that exists. When you are carrying out your coursework, you should always keep in mind that your subjects do not react to things the same way that you do and you must be careful not to impose your *frame of reference* onto them.

victim studies: often used in the study of crime and deviance, these are ways of finding out levels of criminality by asking people which crimes have they had carried out against them. Victim studies are quite a popular area of study in coursework, as the incidence of different types of crime is always of interest to sociologists. Most projects using victim studies will choose to focus on a small area of crime rather than try to cover all types.

vital statistics: official records of the numbers of births, deaths and marriages, collected by the government. Much sociological research begins with these important demographic figures and you are likely to refer to them if you choose to study certain fields of social life, such as the family (see also *hard statistics*).

word limit: the recommended length of your project. Both AQA and OCR AS and A2 specifications identify word limits for sections of your project. While there are no penalties attached to exceeding the word limit, there are no particular advantages in terms of marks either.

A-Z of resources for sociology coursework

1 Organisations which may be helpful in carrying out your coursework

A–Z of sources of information for projects and personal studies

While every effort has been made to ensure the accuracy of this information, organisations do change their addresses and the focus of their activities from time to time. Nearly all the organisations included in this section have their own Websites. It might therefore be a good idea to check the Website of the particular organisation before you write to the address given. We have purposely not given the telephone numbers of these organisations as it is easier to keep a record of your work if the first contact is by letter or e-mail and you keep a copy of it. However, if you choose to make first contact by telephone – you can find the number on the Website – make sure that you record in your research diary what was agreed during your conversation.

Name and address	Area of concern or type of information available
ACAS Brandon House 180 Borough High Street London SE1 2LW	This organisation is concerned with resolving industrial disputes between bosses and workers.
Active Community Unit Home Office 7th Floor 50 Queen Anne's Gate London SW1H 9AT	This is a government-supported initiative to create a climate of active involvement in local communities and important for any community-based coursework.
Advertising Standards Authority 2/16 Torrington Place London WCIE 7HW	May be useful in examining whether advertisements are honest, decent and fair.

Name and address	Area of concern or type of information available
Age Concern Astral House 1268 London Road Norbury London SW16 4ER	A valuable source of information about the position of the elderly in society, from the point of view of a pressure group.
Amnesty International 99–119 Rosebery Avenue London ECIR 4RE	Concerned with human rights issues throughout the world.
Anti-Nazi League PO Box 2566 London N4 1WJ	A left-wing group which opposes racist and extreme right-wing groups. Often involved in direct action.
Association for the Teaching of the Social Sciences (ATSS) PO Box 6079 Leicester LE2 4DW	This organisation represents teachers of sociology in the UK.
BBC Television Television Centre Wood Lane London WI2 7RJ	A massive resource for sociologists interested in the media and especially television and radio.
British Ecological Society 26 Blades Court Deodar Road Putney London SW15 2NU	Concerned with issues to do with the environment; this covers a whole range of issues such as the conservation of wild animals and plants.
British Refugee Council 3 Bondway London SW8 1SJ	Mainly concerned with the rights of asylum seekers.
British Youth Council 2 Plough Yard Shoreditch High Street London EC2A 3LP	A pressure group which aims to represent the views of young people to government and is interested in the minimum wage, citizenship, etc.
Building Societies Association 3 Savile Row London W1S 3PB	A representative body for the traditional mortgage lenders, who support the principle of mutuality.

Campaign for Freedom of Information
Suite 102
16 Baldwins Gardens
London ECIN 7RJ

This campaigning group acts against secrecy and in favour of freedom of information legislation.

Campaign for Press and Broadcasting Freedom (CPBF)
2nd Floor
Vi & Garner Smith House
23 Orford Road
Walthamstow
London E17 9NL

This group campaigns for greater democratic control and accountability in the media.

Campaign for State Education (CASE)
158 Durham Road
London SW20 ODG

A group interested in publicly funded schooling and a fair education system for all children.

CBI (Confederation of British Industry)
Centre Point
100 New Oxford Street
London WC1A IDU

A large employers' association which is a good source of business statistics.

Centre for Citizenship Studies in Education
University of Leicester
21 University Road
Leicester LE1 7RF

Concerned with the promotion of good citizenship in schools; they are active in the campaign for compulsory citizenship lessons.

Centre for the Study of Comprehensive Schools (CSCS)
University of Leicester
Moulton College, Moulton
Northampton NN3 7RR

An organisation which researches into and promotes comprehensive schools, as opposed to selection.

Centrepoint
Neil House
7 Whitechapel Road
London E1 1DU

Provides advice to the homeless and is therefore interested in housing issues.

Child Poverty Action Group
94 White Lion Street
London N1 9PF

A campaigning charity which seeks to lift all children from circumstances of poverty.

A B C D E F G H I J K L M N O P Q R S T U V W X Y Z

Children's Legal Centre
University of Essex
Wivenhoe Park
Colchester CO4 3SQ

Associated with the campaign to institute children's legal rights; also provides the young with advice.

Children's Rights
Development Unit
Chancery House
319 City Road
London EC1V 1LJ

Involved with the issue of children's legal status and rights.

Children's Society
The Edward Rudolf House
69–85 Margery Street
London WCIX OJL

A religious charity which works with some of the most vulnerable young people in society.

Citizen's Charter Unit
Charter Mark and Beacon Unit
Cabinet Office
Admiralty Arch
The Mall
London SW1A 2WH

Concerned with the implementation of charter marks for good public service.

Citizenship Foundation
Ferroners House
Shaftsbury Place
Aldersgate Street
London EC2Y 8AA

An organisation concerned with all aspects of citizens' rights and duties, it publishes a range of useful resources in this area.

Commission for Racial Equality
Elliott House
10–12 Allington Street
London SWIE 5EH

A rich source of material on issues to do with ethnic minorities over a large number of social fields.

Community Development
Foundation
60 Highbury Grove
London N5 2AG

Encourages local people to become involved in their communities and enter partnerships with government and other organisations.

Consumers' Association
2 Marylebone Road
London NWI 4DF

Concerned with marketing issues in a way which seeks to champion the cause of the consumer.

Council for Disabled Children
8 Wakley Street
London ECIV 7QE

Promotes the welfare of the young disabled with a wide variety of conditions.

Council for the Protection of
Rural England
25 Buckingham Palace Road
London SW1W 0PP

A campaigning organisation which
seeks to conserve traditional ways
of life in the countryside.

CVS
(Community Service Volunteers)
237 Pentonville Road
London N1 9NJ

Seeks to challenge young people to
work in local communities on a variety
of projects.

Demos
The Mezzanine
Elizabeth House
39 York Road
London SE1 7NQ

An independent think tank which seeks
to promote long-term and radical
policy initiatives over a wide range of
areas such as identity, information
society and life-long learning.

Development Education Centre
Woodthorpe School
Woodthorpe Road
Sheffield S13 8DD

An independent charity concerned
with education in the issue of
world development.

Electoral Reform Society
6 Chancel Street
London SE1 0UU

An independent expert body
concerned with all things to do
with elections.

Equal Opportunities Commission
Arndale House
Arndale Centre
Manchester M4 3EQ

A government body with a great deal
of information on gender equality
over a wide range of social fields.

Friends of the Earth
26–28 Underwood Street
London N1 7JQ

A campaigning organisation concerned
with all things environmental from
the rainforest to pollution.

Greenpeace
Canonbury Villas
London N1 2PN

An independent organisation associated
with direct action on environmental
issues.

Hansard Society
9 Kingsway
London WC2B 6FX

Exists to promote effective
parliamentary democracy and thus one
of the best sources of material on
democratic participation

Help the Aged
207–221 Pentonville Road
London N1 9UZ

This charity focuses on the needs of
the elderly in society.

A B C D E F G H I J K L M N O P Q R S T U V W X Y Z

Howard League for Penal Reform
1 Ardleigh Road
London NI 4HS

This organisation has many resources on prisons and prison reform. It is an active campaigner for change to the prison system.

Institute of Economic Affairs
Health and Welfare Unit
2 Lord North Street
London SWIP 3LB

This research-based group offers radical views on issues concerned with health and welfare.

Institute for Public Policy Research
30–32 Southampton Street
London WC2E 7RA

An organisation concerned with research into policy issues, such as health and welfare, market issues, etc.

Chartered Institute of Environmental Health
Chadwick House
15 Hatfields
London SE1 8DJ

This is an interesting source of information if you are interested in sociological issues to do with the environment, such as noise pollution.

Institute of Race Relations
2–6 Leeke Street
London WCIX 9HS

An independent organisation which funds research throughout the world into issues of racial justice.

Joseph Rowntree Foundation
The Homestead
40 Water End
York YO30 6WP

Publishes material on the issues of housing, social care and social policy.

Learning Through Action
Fair Cross
Stratfield Saye
Reading RG7 2BT

This is an educational trust which deals with issues such as bullying, drugs and alcohol abuse, parenting, gender and ethnic differences.

Liberty (NCCL)
21 Tabard Street
London SE1 4LA

One of the main organisations associated with civil rights and the protection of the individual from overbearing power.

Local Government Information Unit
22 Upper Woburn Place
London WCIH OTB

A valuable source of information about all the functions carried by local authorities.

Minority Rights Group
379 Brixton Road
London SW9 7DE

This is the section of Amnesty International that seeks to promote the rights of ethnic, linguistic and religious minorities throughout the world.

The National Aids Trust
Publications
New City Cloisters
188/196 Old Street
London EC1V 9FR

Through its campaigning work, this
organisation seeks to promote a cure
for AIDS and to combat discrimination
against people who are HIV-positive or
who have AIDS-related conditions.

National Children's Bureau
8 Wakley Street
London EC1V 7QE

This charity seeks to promote the
interests of young people and combat
their social exclusion.

National Council for One Parent
Families
255 Kentish Town Road
London NW5 2LX

The main support group for lone
parent families, it is a good source of
information on this issue.

National Council for Voluntary
Organisations
Regent's Wharf
8 All Saints Street
London N1 9RL

An umbrella organisation for the
voluntary sector and therefore it has
a wide range of information available.

National Foundation for
Educational Research
The Mere, Upton Park
Slough
Berks SL1 2DQ

A research organisation, producing
many publications concerning
education.

National Society for the Prevention
of Cruelty to Children (NSPCC)
45 Curtain Road
London EC2A 3NH

One of the main children's charities
that is active in the field of child abuse
and ill-treatment.

National Youth Agency
17–23 Albion Street
Leicester LE1 6GD

This has the most comprehensive
resource bank on work with young
people which is available for loan and
inspection.

Newspapers in Education (NIE)
The Newspaper Society
Bloomsbury House
74–77 Great Russell Street
London WC1B 3DA

This organisation promotes a number
of initiatives to encourage the use of
newspapers in educational settings.
It also produces many resources.

Politeia
22 Charing Cross Road
London WC2 0QP

This is a forum for social and economic
thinking covering a wide range of
contemporary political issues.

A
B
C
D
E
F
G
H
I
J
K
L
M
N
O
P
Q
R
S
T
U
V
W
X
Y
Z

Politics Association
Old Hall Lane
Manchester M13 0HR

A main source of information on all things political.

Public Records Office
Ruskin Avenue
Kew, Richmond
Surrey TW9 4DU

This organisation holds the national archives of official documents about a large number of topics.

Quaker Social Responsibility and Education Department
Friends House
173–177 Euston Road
London NW1 2BJ

A source of resources from a particular perspective on housing, social inclusion crime, social justice and the environment.

Relate
Herbert Gray College
Little Church Street
Rugby CV21 3AP

An organisation devoted to supporting marriages and relationships in all their various aspects.

Save the Children
Mary Datchelor House
17 Grove Lane
London SE5 8RD

Combating ill-treatment of children throughout the world, this charity has a wealth of information about the situation of young people.

Scope
6 Market Road
London N7 9PW

This charity seeks to challenge stereotypes of those with cerebral palsy and provides an education service for members of the public.

Stonewall
46–48 Grosvenor Gardens
London SW1W 0EB

An organisation which works for equality and social justice for lesbians, gay men and bisexuals.

Shelter
88 Old Street
London EC1V 9HU

A campaigning organisation around the issue of homelessness. It has many different sections to explore as a resource.

TUC
Congress House
28 Great Russell Street
London WC1B 3LS

The official voice of organised workers, it is a source of much information on work and employment rights.

UNICEF (UK)
Africa House
64–78 Kingsway
London WC2B 2NB

An international organisation which represents the interests of children.

There are other local organisations which may be a source of advice and support: local councils, banks, building societies, housing aid centres, youth service, YMCA/YWCA, social service offices, Samaritans, student welfare officers, emergency services, trading standards offices, consumer advice centres, health authorities and trusts, citizens' advice bureaux, volunteer organisations, political party local branches, public libraries, local newspaper offices and local museums. Local branches of national charities (e.g. Cruise, Gingerbread, Families Need Fathers, Homestart and pre-school playgroups) may be a valuable resource. Your local library should be able to help you make contact with all these groups, or you are likely to find their addresses and numbers in the local telephone directory.

2 Other useful sources of information

National statistics

Incorporating the Office for National Statistics, this body is responsible for the archiving and presentation of all the government statistics produced by various departments. It is also responsible, under the new National Statistician, for ensuring the integrity of the official statistics, obtainable through http://www.statistics.gov.uk. The statistics produced include some important publications each year, which are very useful to the sociological researcher. In particular, the *Annual Abstract of Statistics and Social Trends* are of enormous value to coursework students. They are available in most main libraries and your school or college may have previous or current year's copies.

Sociology Review

This magazine is produced four times a year by Philip Allan Updates. It contains articles and activities on a variety of sociological topics and is aimed specifically at the AS/A2 market. Back copies of *Sociology Review* constitute a very important resource for the coursework student, as they will provide fairly recent material on all topic areas. Your school or college library will be likely to have back copies, or your sociology teacher may be able to arrange access to important articles for you. The magazine is available on subscription from:

Philip Allan Updates
Sociology Review
Market Place
Deddington
Oxon OX15 0SE

Sociology Update

This is an annual production of enormous value to the coursework student, as it provides up-to-date statistics and reviews on the latest developments in sociology. It is organised into topics and is very easy to read. It is available from:

Professor Martyn Denscombe
Sociology Update
32 Shirley Road
Stoneygate
Leicester LE2 3LJ

3 Internet resources

Any list of websites will inevitably only represent a small proportion of the information on sociology that is available. The following list attempts to offer the best way into focused research of the Internet. Remember that website addresses do change and, although these were correct at the time of writing, you may have to be creative in the way you search out any particular site. Try to exploit the power of the Net by using links from one page to another as you search for information.

A B C D E F G H I J K L M N O P Q R S T U V W X Y Z

Website	URL (Internet address)	What the site can provide
Association for the Teaching of the Social Sciences	http://www.atss.org.uk/	There are a number of links to the major sociology sites available on the Net with an emphasis on Advanced level. There are also links to useful non-sociological sites.
Centre for Applied Social Surveys: Question Bank	http://www.scpr.ac.uk/cass	This is an invaluable resource which gives you access to the questions asked in official social surveys through the Question Bank. You may need Acrobat Reader to access these, but this can be downloaded free from the Net.
Classical Sociological Theory	http://www.spc.uchicago.edu/ssr1/PRELIMS/theory.html	Get back to basics, with a chapter-by-chapter summary of the classical sociologists' major works.
Cybersociology	http://www.cybersoc.com/	This will give you access to a number of electronic handouts and essays, especially on cultural studies.
Dave Harris Homepage	http://www.arasite.org/	This will give you access to a number of electronic handouts and essays, especially on cultural studies.
Dead Sociologists Society	http://www.2pfeiffer.edu/~lridener/DSS/INDEX.HTML	This provides information on all the classical sociologists, as well as comprehensive links to other sites.
Hewett School, Norfolk	http://www.hewett.norfolk.sch.uk/curic/soc/index.html	Just one of a growing number of schools which provide on-line access to curriculum support materials for sociologists of Advanced and GCSE levels. This includes an 'Ideas for Coursework' section.

Website	URL (Internet address)	What the site can provide
Sackville Sociology Research Group	http://www.spartacus.schoolnet.co.uk/sociology.report.html	This is an example of a coursework project on under-achievement at GCSE. The report will give you some insight into the problems of research.
Social Science Information Gateway UK (SOSIG)	http://www.sosig.ac.uk/	This is one of the main ways to access resources on the Internet through a listing of sociology sites.
Social World: Sociology	http://www.angelfire.com/ma/Socialworld/Sociology.html	There are an extensive number of links on this page, especially on issues such as postmodernism and culture.
Sociological Research Online	http://www.socresonline.org.uk/socresonline/	The British Sociological Association's electronic journal. Abstracts and articles of new research are available. There are some restrictions with more recent articles.
Sociological Tour Through Cyberspace	http://www.trinity.edu/~mkearl/index.html	All sorts of advice and contacts on this site, such as a 'Guide to writing a research paper' and 'Exercising the Sociological Imagination'. There are also plenty of links on the main topics of the AS/A2 exams.
Sociology at Bryn Hafren School	http://atschool.eduweb.co.uk/barrycomp/bhs/	While this covers general A level and GCSE issues, there is a section on supporting research, which offers guidance to the coursework student.

Website	URL (Internet address)	What the site can provide
Sociology Central	http://www.sociology.org.uk	This is an excellent site maintained by Chris Livesey and giving access to a whole range of downloadable resources, aimed specifically at Advanced level sociology students in Great Britain.
Sociology Classroom	http://home.att.net/~sociologyclassroom/	An American site that has internet resources for High School students and teachers. It is aimed at Year 12 and Year 13 students, with a comprehensive set of links by topic.
Sociology Internet Resources	http://www.wcsu.ctstateu.edu/socialsci/socres.html	This offers a large number of useful links organised by topics.
Sociology Online	http://sociologyonline.co.uk/HomeNot4.html	There are lots of files on sociological topics to look at here, as well as power point presentations and quizzes.
SocioRealm	http://www.digerativeweb.com/sociorealm	Although there is a limited number of topics on this site, it does give you access to search facilities and to other sites recommended by visitors. Make sure you add to it if you visit. There is also sound attached to this site.
Yahoo Index to Sociology Sites	http://www.yahoo.com/social_science/sociology/	This is one of the major search engines available on the web and it categorises sites by subject. This will take you to the list of links for sociology sites.

A B C D E F G H I J K L M N O P Q R S T U V W X Y Z